D0425611

BACKGROUND TO REVOLUTION

The Development of Modern Cuba

Borzoi Books ON LATIN AMERICA

General Editor

LEWIS HANKE

COLUMBIA UNIVERSITY

BACKGROUND TO REVOLUTION

The Development of Modern Cuba

❋ ❋ ❋

EDITED WITH AN INTRODUCTION BY

Robert Freeman Smith

UNIVERSITY OF RHODE ISLAND

New York: Alfred · A · Knopf

L. C. catalog card number: 65–17485

THIS IS A BORZOI BOOK,
PUBLISHED BY ALFRED A. KNOPF, INC.

Copyright © 1966 by Alfred A. Knopf, Inc.
All rights reserved. No part of this book may be reproduced in any form without permission in writing from the publisher, except by a reviewer, who may quote brief passages in a review to be printed in a magazine or newspaper. Manufactured in the United States of America and distributed by Random House, Inc. Published simultaneously in Toronto, Canada, by Random House of Canada Limited.

PUBLISHED, JANUARY 1966,
REPRINTED, 1968

Dedicated to

Herminio Portell Vilá

and *Emilio Roig De Leuchsenring,*

whose pioneering works on U.S.–Cuban relations were too long ignored in the United States.

102972

Acknowledgments

The preparation of this volume has been expedited with the help of various friends. Thomas F. McGann, Lewis Hanke, and José M. Pérez Cabrera provided many useful suggestions; Roland T. Ely and Duvon C. Corbitt most generously sent copies of published material and advised on the selection of articles. The students in Professor Hanke's colloquium on Latin American History at Columbia University in the fall semester of 1964 discussed the manuscript and made several suggestions for its improvement.

I am especially indebted to Arnaldo Sierra for his valuable assistance in translating several of the Cuban selections and to Bill Gard for his translation of the Russian article. The Department of History of the University of Rhode Island co-operated in various ways, and Betty Gard assisted in the typing.

I doubt that I could ever produce a manuscript on time and in readable condition without the varied assistance of my wife Alberta.

ROBERT FREEMAN SMITH

Kingston, R.I.

Contents

BACKGROUND TO REVOLUTION

The Development of Modern Cuba

Introduction

Ignorance and misunderstanding on the part of several nations have, to an important degree, provided the background to revolution in Cuba. Spain, Great Britain, France, the United States, and the Soviet Union have at various times regarded the island as part of their international power structure, and have tried to influence or control its internal developments. This has been especially true during periods of upheaval, and historians can find an interesting similarity in the policies of these outside powers from the conspiracies of the 1820's and 1840's, through the Ten Years War (1868–78), and the revolutions of 1895, 1933, and 1959.

These nations have frequently tried to define the Cuban situation by means of slogans. "Pearl of the Antilles," "the ever-faithful isle," "the ripe apple," "our little ward," and "the beachhead of Marxism-Leninism" have all been utilized as explanations of the island's future and the feelings of its people. Such slogans contain elements of truth, while perpetuating an ignorance of the rest of the Cuban reality. Indeed, the island of stereotypes and slogans has always managed to confound the slogan-makers, often amid cries of betrayal and shouts of indignation from the nation which felt most secure in its relations with Cuba.

This would be of little importance if Cuba had not been involved with empires and their power struggles for most of her recorded history. Cuba's historical development has always been of much importance to one or more outside powers. At various times during the last three centuries such nations as Spain, Great Britain, France, the United States, and Soviet Russia have been affected by events in Cuba. Most of these nations in turn have presented their interpretation of the island's history in order to prove the "true" course of its future. From the beginning of European contact the island has been manipulated by foreign powers that believed Cuba was vital to their interests.

This was due to a combination of factors. Cuba's location, resources, size, insularity, and the nature of its economy have all played a part in the desire and ability of other nations to control it, as well as in the Cuban's own difficulty in trying to limit or break away from foreign influence. But these geopolitical elements are often discussed—especially by foreigners who pontificate about Cuba's "inevitable" destiny or the policy their countries must follow—as if they were completely determining. Although these elements have certainly influenced events, the actions of foreign nations towards Cuba have not been determined by either divine edict or the metaphysics of geopolitics.

The Cuban policies of the various powers have stemmed from the goals and ambitions which their leaders and pressure groups have formulated. These formulations have involved the control or manipulation of Cuba as necessary to national interests as defined by each power. Yet these ambitions, goals, and definitions have all been the product of human decisions based upon what people believed was vital to their economy and security. The geopolitical factors are relative to the way in which policy formulators viewed them and the ambitions which shaped these views. Thus, no nation has had an "inevitable" Cuban policy. This idea itself is a belief based upon other conceptions. The fact that Cuba has been controlled and manipulated by other nations is due not to the working of immutable factors but to decisions and beliefs of men in other nations. In terms of what has happened historically many of these beliefs about Cuba and its role *vis à vis* other powers have not been well grounded in logic or history and the results have often been completely unpredictable.

There are many examples of how policy decisions have been shaped by ideas about Cuba. John Quincy Adams believed that the island was one of the most vital elements in the economic and strategic future of the United States. He wrote:

> Such indeed are, between the interests of that island and of this country, the geographical, commercial, moral, and political relations, formed by nature, gathering in the process of time . . . that in looking forward to the probable course of events for the short period of half a century, it is scarcely possible to resist the conviction that the annexation of Cuba to our federal republic will be indispensable to the continuance and integrity of the Union itself.[1]

Adams was wrong in this analysis. The United States continued to exist without annexing Cuba, and it is extremely doubtful that such a course would have prevented the Civil War. Yet Adams talked about such relations being governed by natural laws. They were governed by Adams and others whose beliefs about economics and strategy and Cuba dictated their policies.[2]

Another factor in the intensification of the sectional controversy in the U.S. was the idea, held by Southern leaders and their political allies, that Cuba was being "Africanized" by British pressure on Spain to abolish slavery. Viewing such a development as a direct threat

---

[1] Secretary of State John Quincy Adams to Hugh Nelson, Minister to Spain, April 28, 1823, W. C. Ford (ed.), *The Writings of John Quincy Adams* (New York, 1913–17), VII, 372–379.

[2] I am not arguing that ideas are autonomous or exist in a vacuum. They are always related to definite interests in shaping foreign policy.

to their socio-economic system, Southerners and their allies stoked the fires of annexation. The so-called Ostend Manifesto declared:

> We should . . . be recreant to our duty . . . should we permit Cuba to be Africanized and become a second St. Domingo, with all its attendant horrors to the white race, and suffer the flames to enter to our own neighboring shores, seriously to endanger or actually to consume the fair fabric of our Union.[3]

"Africanization" was a myth, but it became an active ingredient in a situation which produced expeditions, threats, and intrigue.[4] These in turn compounded the Northern fear of a Great Slave Power Conspiracy to gain political control through expanding the slave labor system. When he rejected the various compromise plans in 1861, Abraham Lincoln voiced this fear as one reason for his action.[5]

Again in 1898 a combination of assumptions, ambitions, and interests prompted American officials to decide on war with a decrepit Spain and a protectorate status for Cuba. To list all the factors involved is beyond the scope of this chapter, but one important belief will suffice as an example. American officials and investors in Cuba did not believe that the Revolutionary government could, or would, govern Cuba in the proper manner—proper, that is, as defined by industrial nations in

---

3 James Buchanan, J. Y. Mason, and Pierre Soulé to William L. Marcy, "The Ostend Conference," October 18, 1854, U.S. Congress, *House Executive Documents,* No. 93, 33d Cong., 2d Sess. (Washington, D.C., 1855), 127–132.

4 C. Stanley Urban, "The Africanization of Cuba Scare, 1853–1955," *Hispanic American Historical Review,* XXXVII (1957), 20–45.

5 Arthur Bestor, "The American Civil War as a Constitutional Crisis," *The American Historical Review,* LXIX (January, 1964), 336.

their relations with underdeveloped areas. General Leonard Wood reported to President William McKinley that:

> People here, Mr. President, know that they are not ready for self government. . . . We are going ahead as fast as we can, but we are dealing with a race that has steadily been going down for a hundred years and into which we have got to infuse new life, new principles and new methods of doing things. This is not the work of a day or of a year but of a longer period.[6]

Thus, the United States became much more involved in the control of Cuba. This control in turn helped to produce much anti-Yankee sentiment and furnished material for the development of a revolutionary "myth."

The historian could also cite Spanish beliefs about Cuba and the influence which these had on her long, expensive efforts to hold the island. In the end Spain was not only impoverished by these efforts, but also lost the remainder of her empire in a war sparked by the Cuban problem. Thus attitudes toward Cuba have affected the foreign powers involved as well as the Cubans.

One could argue that economic, strategic, or geographical factors determined all these events. These factors were involved, but what men have believed to be the Cuban reality has played a prominent role in the decisions. The consequences have been far from salubrious, and in an age when technology leaves little room for error in foreign policy decisions, it is especially vital for world powers to understand the feelings, attitudes, and ideas in the countries that they are involved with diplomatically and economically.

Since outside powers have rarely understood Cuba, their actions have seldom been designed to fit the Cuban

---

[6] Wood to McKinley, April 12, 1900. Leonard Wood MSS., Library of Congress.

situation. Everyone else has presumed to know what was best for the island; all powers have defended their actions on this basis. Solutions and systems have been imposed and devised as if Cuba were putty which could easily be molded into any image.

Cuba's relationship to foreign powers has helped to shape the island's historical development. Only a few other areas in the Western Hemisphere have so consistently lived in the web of power politics and found their courses of action so consistently limited by other nations, and even these have not been the focus of conflict to the same extent as Cuba.[7] Cuban views of foreign relations, as well as Cuban nationalism, reflect this historical legacy.

Some Cubans have always co-operated with outside powers and have benefited from the paternalistic policies of foreign nations. Others have struggled to change the status quo. This has generally involved attempts to break out of the prevailing international power system. Because of this historical pattern of relations with foreign powers, Cubans have tended to identify domestic problems with the policies of the nation which exercises the most influence in Cuba. While this is often an accurate assessment, it has also been exaggerated to explain problems which stemmed from other causes. Due to this same pattern, Cubans have tended to seek the support of outside powers when trying to change political systems, especially if this involved modifying an existing pattern of relations with another power. Cuba's military weakness has often necessitated this search for outside support, but since the new protector has often claimed his pound of flesh as a reward, this has created new problems.

Cuban history is the story of the interplay between external and internal factors, and the culture of modern

[7] Others would be the remaining European colonies, Puerto Rico, Panama, and the island of Hispaniola.

Cuba is its result. While keeping this interaction in mind, the historian cannot ignore the internal elements.

During the latter part of the nineteenth century and the first quarter of the twentieth, Cuba rapidly emerged into the world of industrial technology and finance capitalism with relatively little preparation. The groups which exercised political power after independence were generally unable to make the necessary adjustments; the result was a continuing pattern of struggle for power, attempted reform, and revolutionary potential.

The difficulty of making the needed socio-economic adjustments was partly due to the complete disruption between 1868 and 1929 of a relatively stable socio-economic pattern. The struggle to overthrow Spanish rule between 1868 and 1898 divided Cubans into antagonistic factions and resulted in much destruction of property and loss of life. At the same time industrial technology hit the sugar economy with full force. For the next several decades the small mill owner and farmer were locked in a desperate battle for survival with those who had the capital required for the modern *centrales,* railroads, and expanded land holdings. This process was accelerated after the Spanish-Cuban-American War as North Americans took advantage of depressed land prices, economic chaos, and the guaranteed security offered by the U.S. government to buy sugar mills and land. The large corporation had also moved onto the scene, replacing the individual entrepreneur. Completing the process in the 1920's, North American banks became the vital source of capital.

In 1903, Manuel Sanguily made a prophetic judgment on these developments:

> As this authentic economic revolution develops, it will be followed by a social and political revolution; that is, the transformation of our territorial wealth through changing ownership will result in

> powerful foreign influences on our daily life. Our language will become eroded, discredited, and adulterated. Ultimately, Cuba will be confronted with frightful legal problems and complications which it will be useless to lament and which we shall be powerless to solve, and we shall suffer the painful loss of our national integrity.[8]

Perhaps this expression was too fatalistic, but the economic revolution did have profound consequences. A revolution in land tenure produced a high concentration of land ownership and rendered landless or dependent an important segment of the rural population. Some of the displaced drifted to the cities to comprise a growing urban proletariat as well.

Another element in the disruptive process was the rapid growth of slavery during the nineteenth century. The old Spanish slave code rapidly eroded under the impact of large numbers of slaves and the drive for profit. As a result, the relationship between whites and blacks was more dehumanized. Moreover, a large number of Negroes had not become Cubanized by the time slavery was abolished in the 1880's. The latter problem was compounded between 1912 and 1924, when approximately 230,000 contract laborers were imported from Haiti and Jamaica.

Cuba in the twentieth century had a highly "invertebrate" society. Social cohesion was minimal, since the institutions which normally performed the unifying function—the Church, army, national government, or other conscious social groupings—had either been severely weakened or were new creations. The dominant feature of the economy, the sugar *latifundia,* did not possess even the traditional ties of the feudal land systems in other parts of Latin America, and capitalism, with its

---

[8] Quoted in Ramiro Guerra y Sánchez, *Sugar and Society in the Caribbean* (New Haven, 1964), p. 75.

preponderant elements of foreign control, was to many Cubans synonymous with the new latifundia system.

There was sharp antagonism between the Spaniards who remained in Cuba—often in important positions in commerce and the Church—and those Cubans who had fought for independence. This division weakened the leadership potential of the upper class, and the aristocratic ideals inherited from the nineteenth century complicated both the problems of leadership and social unity. The *Creole* aristocracy, evolving since the late eighteenth century, contained some men of ability. By and large, however, the Cuban Creoles were ill prepared for leadership, since Spain had given them little political power or responsibility.

In spite of these problems a revolutionary leadership had emerged, and a unifying mystique of national loyalty was developing between 1868 and 1898. The United States disrupted these by taking over the independence movement and imposing a settlement which, in many instances, was completely alien to existing traditions. Some Cubans tried to pick up the pieces after 1902, but the momentum, the enthusiasm, and the integrity of the revolutionary movement had been too far eroded. The all too slender chain of national goals, ideals, and leadership had been broken. The threads had been woven by José Martí, Carlos Manuel de Céspedes, Ignacio Agramonte, Antonio Maceo, Máximo Gómez, Calixto García, Bartolomé Masó, and others during thirty years of conflict. The Cubans would try to knit some of the strands into a new social unity, but they were not always in harmony with North American traditions.

Thus during a century in which other Latin American countries were struggling to build independent societies, Cuba experienced the full brunt of colonial rule and the destructive force of a prolonged, violent conflict to end Spanish control. Cubans in the twentieth century then faced the difficult task of molding a social order from the remnants of the previous century, a task complicated by foreign tutelage, the nature of the economy, and social disunity.

José Martí wrote in 1891:

> The scorn of our formidable neighbor, who does not know us, is the greatest danger for our America; and it is imperative that our neighbor know us, and know us soon, so she shall not scorn us, for the day of the visit is at hand. Through ignorance, she might go so far as to lay hands on us. From respect, once she came to know us, she would remove her hands. . . . Nations should have a pillory for whoever fans useless hates; and another for whoever does not tell them the truth in time.[9]

Have the scholars and writers of the United States told "the truth in time"? There is some evidence that they have not.

Scholars certainly bear an important share of the blame. For years the study of Cuba has been assiduously neglected. Prior to the upheaval in 1959, only a small group bothered to investigate an island which had long been proclaimed as vital to American interests. Irene A. Wright, Charles Chapman, Russell Fitzgibbon, William A. Stokes, Duvon C. Corbitt, Lowry Nelson, and a few others kept the flame of Cuban studies alive in this country. All too often, even these efforts were ignored by other writers.

Of perhaps even greater importance, much that was written about Cuba by scholars and journalists was distorted, especially textbooks and works for popular consumption. Ignorance played an important part in these distortions, as did feelings of superiority and even racism. The results have been tragic.

For years too many North Americans saw Cuba as a place where loose women in tight skirts entertained

---

[9] José Martí, "Our America," in Juan de Onís (trans.), *The America of José Martí* (New York, 1953), 150.

tourists in swank casinos; or where men smoking fragrant cigars sold filthy pictures on street corners. Havana cigars, Bacardí Rum, sugar, Sloppy Joe's bar, and San Juan Hill were all mixed up to the rhythm of a cha-cha beat played by people in funny hats. Why did Americans assume that in some way the U.S. owned Cuba? After all, it seemed perfectly natural for U.S. ships to be in a U.S. naval base in Cuba, and for U.S. destroyers to sail into Cuban ports as if they were branch-offices of the Guantánamo establishment. No one ever said this in so many words; it was simply a lasting impression obtained from schoolbooks, teachers, and magazines.[1] Is it any wonder, then, that over the years Americans have been so ill-prepared for developments in Cuba?

Since the nineteenth century North American writings about Cuba have helped to feed the illusions of innocence and omnipotence which form part of the ideological baggage of U.S. foreign policy. Cuba became a symbol of North American righteousness as writers pointed out that independence, prosperity, and security were gifts conferred by the U.S. upon the island. On the other hand, since the United States had never been seriously threatened by Cuba, many North Americans assumed that the influence of the U.S. in Cuba was a normal condition requiring little thought, effort, or understanding. An important element in U.S. reaction to Fidel Castro was his attack on America's illusions of her innocence and omnipotence.

The things that have been written about Cuba by North Americans have in many cases deeply insulted Cuban pride. The United States not only took over the Cuban Revolution in a physical sense, but in an intellectual sense as well. They labeled it the Spanish-American

[1] This is based on my voyage to Cuba on a U.S. Navy destroyer, plus a re-examination of my basic education. This situation has, if anything, become worse since 1959. I often encounter students using the possessive case when discussing Cuba.

War, and North American historians and journalists have promulgated a version of the conflict which eliminates the Cubans almost entirely. The 1963 revision of a leading, basic text in U.S. history states: "It is an exaggeration to speak of the disorder in Cuba that broke out in 1895 as a revolution. . . . Maximo Gomez . . . was utterly unable to maintain a government, or even to keep an army in the field."[2] This is the *last* mention of Cubans in this discussion of the war. The author also perpetuates false historical mythology by praising Walter Reed and William C. Gorgas for their conquest of yellow fever. The Cuban who discovered the means of transmission and finally convinced the U.S. Army doctors of the validity of his theory is never mentioned. Carlos J. Finlay continues to be excluded from North American texts, just as the Surgeon General of the U.S. Army excluded him from the article which he wrote on yellow fever for the *Encyclopaedia Americana* (the article was reprinted without change for half a century). Perhaps the Surgeon General was vexed because, in desperation, Reed and Gorgas ignored his orders to disregard Finlay's theory. But his account is still repeated to American school children.[3]

Cuban historians have written many books trying to correct the record and restore the Cuban heritage of the Revolution. Few scholars in North America read them. In failing to do so they not only perpetuate the version glorifying the U.S. but they also remain ignorant of its effect on Cuban nationalism. Few leading texts in U.S. diplomatic history cite any works by Cubans or utilize any of the research done by these scholars. The most recent book-length study of the "Spanish-American War" does not refer to a single Cuban source and hardly

---

[2] John D. Hicks, *et al.*, *The American Nation*, 4th ed. (Boston, 1963), p. 276.

[3] Letter from Duvon C. Corbitt to the author, July 30, 1964. See Document 4 by Professor Corbitt for additional information.

mentions the Cubans at all except in deprecatory terms.[4] In this respect Professor Samuel Flagg Bemis deserves credit for changing the name of the war in the 1959 edition of his *Short History of American Diplomacy,* and acknowledging the role of Cuban historians in this change.[5]

Meanwhile, Cubans reading the works of their historians were finding out such things as the role of the Revolutionary Army in clearing landing areas so the U.S. Army could straggle ashore for days with no opposition. Is it any surprise that sensitive Cubans wondered why all the efforts of their heroes were studiously ignored in North America? Could it be that in so rewriting the story the Yankees were in effect preparing the historical justification for control, tutelage, and influence? This is exactly what many Cubans believed.

Perhaps the Cubans have been too sensitive, but they reacted as a small, young nation struggling to create and maintain a sense of national identity while living in the shadow of a giant power to the North. One can imagine what the reaction in the young United States would have been if France had taken over the American Revolution, refused to let George Washington participate in the British surrender at Yorktown, set up a military government, and retained Newport, R.I., as a naval base. Then, if French historians had ignored the Continental Army, called the struggle the Franco-British War, and emphasized only the French role, it is entirely conceivable that the American reaction would have been quite similar to Cuba's.[6]

Written history has a definite influence on subsequent historical developments. North American reactions to

---

[4] Frank Freidel, *The Splendid Little War,* (Boston, 1958).

[5] Bemis, p. 275. The title "Spanish-Cuban-American War" was officially sanctioned by the Cuban Congress in 1946.

[6] The intensity of American fears of French ambitions in North America during the 1790's provides some comparison.

events in Cuba have in part been shaped by North American beliefs about Cuba and her history. On the other side of the Florida Straits, the reaction of Cuban intellectuals to Yankee versions of their history became a part of the nationalist ideology and the revolutionary mystique. The events had taken place and could not be corrected, but the insults kept old memories fresh and opened new wounds.

Today as never before historical perspective is needed to counteract simplistic views of world events which can only lead to a frenzy of destruction. Modern Cuba must be viewed in such perspective in order to avoid unrealistic, utopian policies in U.S.–Cuban relations. The following selections are often introductions to subjects which need much more investigation. It is to be hoped that they may serve as a step on the journey to understanding and further study, as well as a contribution to mutual respect between the two nations.

I

❁ ❁ ❁

IDEAS, IDEOLOGIES, AND ATTITUDES

1

C. A. M. HENNESSY

❃

The Roots of Cuban Nationalism

Nationalism, with its emotional and intellectual currents, provides one of the most dynamic forces in modern history. The results differ from country to country, however, since the particular forms that nationalism takes are structured by the historical development of each country. Thus Professor C. A. M. Hennessy bases the following essay on the assumption that recent events in Cuba cannot be interpreted in the context of general statements about Latin American nationalism. According to Hennessy, "Unless . . . the Castro Revolution is seen as a particular type of nationalist upheaval, closely conditioned by Cuban history, there is a danger that false analogies will be made with revolutionary situations elsewhere in Latin America."

Professor Hennessy is Senior Lecturer in history at the University of Warwick (England) and is the

---

From C. A. M. Hennessy, "The Roots of Cuban Nationalism," *International Affairs,* XXXIX (July 1963), 346–358. Reprinted by permission of the Royal Institute of International Affairs and the author.

author of *The Federal Republic in Spain, 1868–74.* He is an active promoter of Latin American studies in England.

A long gestation before independence was not enough in itself to give Cuban nationalism a sense of balance. The absence of a telluric basis for it tended to crystallize nationalist sentiment round the figure of Martí as it has also been a reason why the dynamic behind Cuban nationalism has often seemed to be little more than a febrile, hysterical anti-Americanism. It accounts, too, for the way in which, in Cuba, national myth-making has often lost touch with political reality. This was shown when the nationalists of the 1890's were prepared to devastate the island and so create the conditions for United States intervention rather than accept Spanish reforms. It has been shown, too, in Castro's own brand of nationalism when, on occasions, he has seemed prepared to invite the apotheosis of national martyrdom in the holocaust of a new war. There is also the fact that Cuban nationalism, whether in Martían or Castroist form, has always been couched in Latin American and universalist terms, not those of a narrow Cubanism. That is why the Castro revolution has seen itself as having the messianic mission of "turning the Cordillera of the Andes into the Sierra Maestra of Latin America."

. . .

Any analysis of Cuban nationalism must begin with a consideration of the island's social structure, not only because it has determined the form that nationalism has taken, but also because, in the case of Cuba, the axiom that nationalist movements are fomented, led, and supported by the middle class needs some qualification. What middle class existed in the 19th century consisted of Spanish immigrants who, living in tight urban groups, failed to become assimilated, monopolized commerce, acted as bankers to debt-ridden *criollo* planters and were naturally a main support of the colonial régime. National independence was the objective of a small number of criollo lawyers, writers, liberal priests, and students. Alienated intellectuals, rooted in no social class, make an early début in Cuban history but, unable to convert any but a small number of landowners to the idea of independence, and despised by the Spanish middle class, they were either forced into exile, like Varela (1787–1853) and Saco (1797–1879), or, like Luz y Caballero (1800–1862) and Mendive (1821–1886), they accepted the patient task of educational preparation. The few schools and the University of Havana, after its secularization in 1842, almost entirely criollo staffed, became hothouses of nationalist sentiment.

Yet the decisive impetus to nationalism did not come from these elements but from radical landowners in Oriente who, for mainly economic reasons, revolted against Spanish rule in 1868 and thus began the Ten Years' War. That war was, in essence, the expression of a new nationalism which developed in response to the embittered frustrated nationalism of a declining imperial power which regarded Cuba as an integral part of Spain, and which refused to recognize her separate identity. Absence of easily exploitable wealth, and a small indigenous population had discouraged any intensive Spanish colonization of the island until after Spain had lost her mainland possessions. The economic boom and the sugar revolution of the early 19th century kept Cuba loyal, but this loyalty was rewarded only with relentless political and economic exploitation.

Nevertheless, the war ended in a stalemate because the Oriente landowners failed to win over the wealthier planters in the rest of the island, whose ideology, whether annexationism, reformism or autonomism, was always conditioned by fear of the democratic implications of the nationalists' creed.

The Oriente rebels were, in any case, themselves divided over the implications of the abolition of slavery, and it was only after the war had destroyed the economic basis of the slave system, and with it slavery itself, that this main inhibiting factor in the nationalist revolution was removed. By that time, however, the initiative in the struggle for independence had passed to a small but vocal group of Cubans in Havana and in exile.

. . .

The particular significance of Martí in the history of Cuban nationalism lies in his appearance in the depressed 1880's, at the moment when the nationalist forces were leaderless and divided, and when the abolition of slavery made it feasible, for the first time, to create a mass nationalist movement which would draw its strength from groups other than discontented planters.

. . .

In Martí's populist creed the political nation was all-embracing: his notion of class harmony may have derived from a mystical sense of the brotherhood of all men, but it was also the result of an acute awareness that Cuba had no revolutionary class strong enough to bring a nationalist revolt to fruition. But, however useful in creating a sense of unity against the Spaniards, the populist myth collapsed in the bitter divisions of the early years of independence. The War of Liberation was not the short, sharp struggle which Martí had imagined would forestall United States' intervention, and in which a mass uprising would both overthrow Spanish power and temper a new nationalist spirit. Instead, it dragged on for three years and ended in the foreign intervention which he had so much feared.

Yet it is doubtful if even Martí could have conjured national unity out of the devastation of a three years' war of extermination, or if he would have been able to prevent those developments which were to determine Cuba's future as a monoculture economy. United States capital restored the sugar industry but at the price of perpetuating the latifundia and reducing the small cane planters to complete dependence on foreign-owned mills. Martí believed that political and economic independence were inseparable, and he had argued that Cuban democracy must be based on a small-holding peasantry in a diversified economy. Instead, a relentless process of centralization extended the great sugar estates of the colonial period, thus inhibiting the growth of a rural middle class and creating a landless, agrarian proletariat.

The alienation of the rural proletariat from the land was paralleled by the alienation of the middle sectors from a dynamic role in the state. The neocolonial economy of the Republic left little room for the development of a Cuban middle class. There was no wholesale exodus of Spaniards, and those who remained kept their Spanish citizenship and pre-empted the best posts in the Church and commerce, while a deficient education system rendered many Cubans unfit for technical posts in expanding United States concerns. They could turn only to politics, government service, the professions, and teaching. The social system of the Republic perpetuated the Spanish legacy that public office should be made a source of private profit. Politics thus became the key to social advancement, and so little more than a squabble between factions for the ownership of government. Parties cut across group interests, and *personalismo* rather than principle determined party alignments. Implicit agreements that parties should alternate in power, and thus share out offices, broke down and *continuismo* became the main cause of "revolution" as in 1905, 1917, and after 1928. But that type of "revolution" meant merely a switch of government personnel, not a fundamental social or political change. Perhaps the most striking example of the spoils system was shown in 1948 when Prío Socorrás replaced Grau San Martín as president. Although both were members of the same party, ten thousand government posts nevertheless changed hands.

Government was, in fact, like the lottery which used to play such a prominent part in Cuban politics. Public life was permeated by a boom psychosis, with the middle sectors bidding against each other for government sinecures. In purely economic terms there might have been a middle class, but in terms of self-identification and bourgeois culture values a middle class scarcely existed. Instead, there were what the Cubans themselves describe as the *"capas medias."* There was no strong bourgeois tradition to offset the *rentier* mentality which was one of the main legacies of the criollo plantocracy. Neither anticlericalism nor anti-Americanism gave homogeneity to these groups, whose factionalism was the bane of Cuban politics. Living beyond their means to attain upper class status, patronizing an enormous number of private schools, to the detriment of public education, and bombarded by the advertisements of a consumer society, they lived in a continual state of economic frustration and near-revolutionary ferment, plotting the overthrow of the political structure in order to hasten their accession to the upper reaches of the graft system.

The most coherent section, as might be expected, were the professional groups and the students. The common Latin American phenomenon of the underemployed intellectual can be related to the cultural legacy of the colonial régime, embalmed in a formalistic, literary and nonscientific university system. Critics, like Pozos Dulces (1809–77), Martí, and Varona (1849–1933), who argued that the educational system was totally unrelated to Cuba's needs, were voices crying in the wilderness. Law and medicine were the most oversubscribed professions, the one as a prelude to politics, the other because of its high status value. Although the rural areas desperately needed doctors, a disproportionate number remained in Havana where the opportunities for advancement lay.

The inability of society to absorb the products of the higher educational system exaggerated the dichotomy between generals and doctors. *Caudillismo* based on the power of the army was not an evil of Cuban government until 1933. The disbanding of the army of liberation, under United States' pressure in 1900, prevented it from filling the political vacuum during the early years of independence, as had so often happened on the mainland, and its generals were forced to seek alternative ways of capitalizing their prestige. Even after it was re-established in 1909, the army did not itself act as a political force. The generals, however, expecting to dominate politics by right, did so through manipulation of a patronage system in which lawyers were able to share in the pickings. Zayas, president between 1921 and 1925, represented the new symbiosis where the astute lawyer-politician managed a vast graft system in which generals were cobeneficiaries. Thus not even professional groups were united in their opposition to the status quo, and it was left to the rootless younger generation, faced with a bleak prospect as underemployed intellectuals, to provide the dynamic for a new nationalist conception of culture and politics.

The ideas of the University Reform movement had fallen on fertile ground in Havana University which, with its professors who did little or no work, was a microcosm of the graft in Cuban public life. From 1924, when students forced academic reforms on the government and began extension classes among the poor in the *Universidad Popular José Martí,* the University became both the focus of a regenerative movement and a centre of revolutionary politics. It was this lost generation of students, exiles in their own land, who rediscovered Martí with his nostalgic yearning for an idealized *patria* and his exile's vision of a socially united, racially harmonious, and economically independent country. His stature grew as the expansion of United States cultural and economic influence brought a note of urgency to the intellectuals' search for national identity.

The concept of the "frustrated revolution" of 1895 now helped to explain the contrast between Martí's dream of a rejuvenated nation and the reality of graft and corruption. In this interpretation, United States intervention, rather than the legacies of Spanish rule or indigenous weaknesses, was responsible for the distortions in public life, and for the diversion of Cuban history from the course which Martí had mapped out.

. . .

The Cuban belief that Spanish power had already been broken by the time the United States intervened in 1898, three years after the beginning of the War of Liberation, gave a keen edge to anti-Americanism, and the coincidence of national independence with a new phase of American imperialism made for an easy transference of nationalist antagonism from Spain to the United States. The attribution of all internal shortcomings to foreign intervention prevented a more fundamental analysis of the new republic's social *malaise*. There was also the fact that economic control from the United States, being more insidious than political control from Spain, precluded the possibility of heroic action.

After the postwar sugar boom broke in the early 1920's, American banks secured a dominant position in the sugar industry economy. By the late 1920's American interests controlled seventy percent of sugar production and had become the financial prop of the unpopular régime of President Machado (1925–1933). The humiliating Platt Amendment and the repercussions of the 1929 crisis made anti-Americanism a main ingredient in the revolutionary movement which finally drove him from power in 1933. The revolutionary government of Grau San Martín, a university professor supported by university students, represented the radical nationalism of frustrated intellectuals, but it could rally little coherent support in the country at large. It was only to be expected that the United States would not recognize a régime which threatened nationalization, but more significant was the hostility in Cuba itself of the two other revolutionary elements, organized labor, which was partly under Communist domination, and Batista's newly promoted ex-sergeant officer corps.

Grau's reaction to the frustrated revolution of 1933 was to organize the nearest thing to a mass party in Cuban politics since Martí's P.R.C. Adopting the same name (although popularly known as the *Auténticos*), this party deliberately appealed more widely than to a specifically middle-sector audience. But even so, Batista's power condemned him to ten years of opposition. Ruling first through a succession of puppet presidents, and from 1940 to 1944 as president himself, Batista, supported by United States business interests, a pampered army, and a tamed labor movement, could afford to ignore Grau whose potential nationalist support had been siphoned off by the Cubanization law of 1933 (which compelled firms to employ 50 percent Cuban personnel), by the abrogation of the Platt Amendment in 1934 as part of Roosevelt's Good Neighbor policy, by the desperation of terrorist groups, like Guiteras' *Joven Cuba* which had been caught up in the mystique of violence, and by Batista's own brand of popular nationalism.

If Cuban reformers were frustrated during the 1934–40 period, at least this could be explained in terms of Batista's corporate-style dictatorship. After 1944, when the Auténticos were in power, explanations were more difficult. Why did a revolutionary party fail to implement the neo-Socialist constitution of 1940 introduced by Batista, under left-wing pressure as the Communists have claimed, in order to revive his waning popularity? Grau's failure to break the pattern of corruption, and even his extension of it into the labor movement in an effort to smash the Communist hold on the unions, discredited his party and led, in 1947, to the formation of a splinter party, the *Ortodoxos.* This now became the repository of revolutionary virtue and the refuge of yet another rootless younger generation. Although the Communists had attracted intellectuals of the caliber of Marinello, few were prepared to accept that particular type of discipline which, in the 1930's, demanded working agreements with Batista in preference to the democratic Left.

The failure of the Auténticos reflected the personalities of its leaders, the whittling down of radical programs through a need for working alliances in Congress, failure to stem graft and internal factionalism. It was a disaster for Cuba because it widened the sphere of corruption, further divided the middle sectors in the splintering of both Auténticos and Ortodoxos after 1952, and bred a cynicism about the abilities of Cubans to make democracy work. . . .

. . .

Throughout the frustrating 1930's and 1940's the Martí cult gathered adherents, although an ambivalent attitude towards his writings reflected the divisions within the middle sectors where his popularity was greatest. The cult betrayed many of the characteristics of a sect mentality, providing a psychological compensation for a middle class lacking both power and faith in its own ability to change a society corrupted by United States' influences. It provided a flight into a world of fantasy where, in the style of Rodo's *Ariel,* Cuban spirituality was contrasted with United States' materialism and greed. But Martí's message became smothered in a torrent of words from those seeking a justification for present policies or a solace for past failures. Never was this more evident than in 1953, Martí's centenary and the first year of Batista's dictatorship, when over five hundred articles on Martí were published. In contrast, there were those like Castro, to whom Martí was primarily a man of action, and for whom the cult provided not only the utopian vision behind the revolutionary movement but also a sense of continuity with the past and thus a means of identification with the heroic period of Cuba's history.

2

WILLIAM REX CRAWFORD

❋

The Development of Cuban Thought

During the nineteenth century Cuba produced several intellectual giants. These men provided much of the philosophical capital for the Cuban nation, since they interpreted the main currents of Western thought for several generations of Cubans. One of the most significant common denominators which emerges from a consideration of these men is the lack of any rigid ideological structure. The fluidity of the Cuban intellectual tradition can, in part, be traced to the influence of these men.

The book from which this selection is taken has been for many years the standard work on Latin American thought. William Rex Crawford, who had a long and distinguished career on the faculty of the University of Pennsylvania, was a pioneer among U.S. scholars in this field.

From William Rex Crawford, *A Century of Latin American Thought,* rev. ed. (Cambridge, Mass., Harvard University Press, 1941, 1961), pp. 218–223, 232–236. Reprinted by permission of the publisher.

In addition to the revered revolutionary leader José Martí, Cuba can point with pride to a number of distinguished thinkers and with pious care has studied them. The incorruptible Father Varela not only was the first modern teacher of philosophy in Cuba, apologizing in 1824 for finding himself under the necessity of attacking scholasticism, but is credited with having taught Cubans to think and having aroused them to the realities of their social situation. In the Cuba of his time these activities eventually led to difficulties, and Father Varela spent the last half of his life in the United States, editing his review *El Habanero* until 1826, and later, with Saco, *El Mensajero Semanal,* and becoming a well-known figure in liberal ecclesiastical circles. His inability to separate his religious principles from his respect for human freedom make him a memorable figure of colonial Cuba, and his mission to innovate bore fruit that he did not live to see.

With something less of revolutionary zeal, Luz has been attacked in some quarters as less than a true patriot. He was, in any case, a great educator and trainer of teachers. His successor in the chair of philosophy, the more versatile and influential Varona, had only high praise for his teaching.

Saco, too, is a figure around whom controversy has centered. Soto Paz, with some vehemence, lists the reasons for regarding his glorification as excessive, and calls him slave-owner, anti-abolitionist, defeatist, and opponent of separation from the mother country; man without a country. With more reason, his followers in the respected Economic Society—which has always stood for realism, industry, and progress—applaud his solid merits, his magnificent writing—less rhetorical and better informed and documented than was customary in his period—his sincerity, balance, powers as an analyst and historian, his energy as a thinker and polemist. Impossible to classify except by applying the elastic term sociologist, Saco knew his country, thought through her problems, looked into her future, and recorded her past. One of his own statements, made in 1862, shows that he knew himself, too, and reveals the reason for his curiously mixed reputation. "I cannot reconcile myself to the political maxim, all or nothing; instead, I am guided by its contrary, if not all, then something at least." He did want the best for his people, but he knew the difficulties and was less sanguine of quick success than more enthusiastic but less informed thinkers. He wrote the history of slavery and desired its abolition, but knew that abolition would bring problems, and that the time had to be ripe. He chafed under Spanish misrule, but thought an adjustment with Spain might be made, and admitted that complete independence would be difficult to achieve unaided and in view of the apathy of many Cubans; so in a famous paper on annexation he held the whip of possible annexation to the United States over Spain's head. Not desiring incorporation in the American republic, he still knew that it might become necessary and was prepared to make the best of it. In the meantime, judicious mention of the possibility might help secure a solution more to his liking. Reform, but peaceably and within the limits of proved possibility, is his aim. Such reasonableness, in 1848 or any other year, is not calculated to rouse the wild enthusiasm of Latin Americans.

. . .

If [Enrique José] Varona is not better known to us and to all of Latin America, it is for interesting reasons. Except in literary criticism, where his interest was catholic, he limited himself almost entirely to Cuban matters. His solutions for domestic problems were not always followed, however. Varona was so superior in his culture, so austere in his political morality, so much a man of balance and *mesure* that he perhaps missed the following and the political success we would wish for him. He rose to be vice-president of the Republic, was to an incomparable degree the teacher of his people, provided a rationale and a goal for their social and political course. To lead a people forward on the path of civilization one must be more than a specialist, and Varona multiplied himself and his activities to an astonishing degree, teaching, admonishing, and writing on a wide variety of subjects, and so prolifically that his bibliography swells to 1880 items. All of this makes him one of the highest specimens of the intellectual life of the island; but note the word, "specimen," and remember that Latin America does not use anything so colorless or inactive for its great heroes of the sword or pen.

Varona is credited with having introduced positivism into Cuba, with being one of its great exemplars in the whole of Latin America. True enough, he did admire many things about Comtism; he did distrust metaphysics and believe that Latin America had suffered from excess of theology and "literature"; he did call for the development of the scientific spirit and for investigation. But although his thought was orderly, he was not seduced by systems, and was enough the independent thinker to reject parts of Comte's teaching and to follow other guides as well: Spencer, Schäffle, Lilienfeld, Ward, Giddings, Tarde, Durkheim. There is no question that the name of Positivist has stuck to him, however, and one reads between the lines that this fact is not unrelated to the bogging down of the project to publish his collected works at the end of the fourth volume.

For us, Varona refuses to be forcibly adjusted to the Procrustean bed of positivism, or any other. No single label describes the man. No single sentence sums him up, unless it be one that Rodó wrote him: "You might be the Próspero of my book." Even within the realm of his philosophy alone we must distinguish two Varonas, two periods or modes of thought. In one aspect he is "academic, systematic, optimistic"; in the other "vital, fragmentary, organic, skeptical." When we step over the boundaries of one discipline to attempt a summary of his whole evolution we find useful guidance in Entralgo's chronological scheme. In his first phase, say from 1879, he is liberal, positivistic, reminds us of Lastarria; after 1885, the influence of Spencer is dominant, and he is in all things the evolutionist and the psychologist, but more pessimistic than the English writer. Utilitarianism and economics attract him after 1899, and we conclude that he has been reading a good deal of John Stuart Mill. With the coming of the World War his pessimism and skepticism reach new depths, and it is the pacifist, the nihilist, the admirer of Montaigne and of Anatole France who speaks to us in aphorisms as bitter and disappointed as any we can find in Latin-American books.

Such a summary helps us to picture Varona. The Cuban sociologist, Agramonte, contributes another, according to which the master emerges as anti-metaphysical, an evolutionist, an advocate of a philosophy based on science, a negator of religion who sees in it only a consolation, not a system of truth; a sympathizer with Rousseau and with the newer trends in education—empirical in his logic, physiological and sensualist in his psychology; a relativist and individualist in ethics; in sociology one who has a clear and penetrating vision of the social whole; a persistent doubter of the possibility of history; in literary taste fundamentally intellectual and romantic in spite of the polished classicism of his form.

Medardo Vitier adds to the picture a note on Varona's tolerance, his remarkable ability to summarize the ideas of others and present them sympathetically, his lifelong intellectual curiosity, which resulted in a vast and varied erudition, his sunny southern clarity, his love of the truth, even when it led to frank heterodoxy.

When one remembers that Varona's eloquence impressed his hearers as overwhelming, and that as the presiding genius of *La Revista cubana* he shaped its policies and spoke to the mind and conscience of Cuba's élite, it is evident that we are dealing with a figure of the first magnitude, one of the glories of Hispanic American thought and writing.

In the *Homenaje* to Varona, unfortunately delayed in appearing until after his death, Vitier applauds the position taken by Varona, eminently a man of the humanities and of philosophy, toward the university. Cuban youth, he held, should look less exclusively toward the university and more toward industrial and mercantile life; he pled for natives of the island to go into business and industry, to show more ambition and exploit the resources of their land by hard work and enterprises started and managed by Cubans. The reaction against a purely literary education has started, but the fruits of the reaction ripen slowly. Asked to summarize Varona's civic teaching, he stresses the demand for civic virtue and criticism of its lack; Cubans have too much tendency to appear publicly satisfied with their government, and to grumble in private. Another unfortunate trait is their love of ostentation and of living beyond their means, which is related to the desire to make profits quickly and by any means whatever—their preference of gambling to the painfully slow results of hard work. Varona not only preached against such stumbling blocks on the road to national greatness; "his whole life was the incarnation of an attitude . . . toward the various problems of his country," and he was the mentor and consultant of two generations. Consultants, to be sure, do not speak with clarion voice, are not agitators or inciters to rebellion; Varona is apollonian, not dionysiac; he failed to communicate and to arouse, and so he is respected, but not popular—a potential Próspero, who for some reason failed to write the great works and lead the great movements; and he is more likely to lie in the cold hard bed of the "classic" than to lie in the hearts of men.

. . .

Called to a messiahship, [José] Martí was more the man of action, less the man of science than Varona; there were no hesitations, no reserves, no qualifications in his affirmations and negations. But he was also an artist and an intellect fertile in ideas. Ideas were for him weapons in the fight for a better world, in which freedom for Cuba was the first step. To preach this gospel and to redeem America, this was his obsession and his mission.

The wealth of ideas in Martí is almost entirely related to this central theme; he had little patience with literature without a social message. The characteristics of man and message have led to no little controversy among worshipers and students of Martí, who have called him now romantic, now the least romantic of leaders, have tried to claim him for Marxism, and have denied the similarity of his views to orthodox socialism or communism. These followers have used him to bolster their anti-United States emotions, and have found in him support for friendly collaboration with the northern republic.

While the imposition of system upon a body of thought that was not systematic would be an error, it seems possible to find a statement which will convey the essential attitude of Martí. He was a mystic, but a practical one; a utopian but at the same time a realist. He took up again the dreams of freedom and union that had been dreamed by Bolívar and inspired others with them. He hoped for a benevolent attitude on the part of the United States, and eventually for some kind of union in the whole Hemisphere, but never for a situation in which Latin America would be the vassal. The United States and Latin America represent two differing, and incomplete, conceptions of life; each can learn from the other. As they learn to know each other, each will come to understand and even to incorporate in its culture what the other has to offer. . . .

. . .

On the question of his economic ideas, it behooves us to remember that Martí was no follower of another man's system, and that the keynote of his own thought was love, for love, he said, is the only force that builds, and the only ethical justification of force. What he took from other ideologists was assimilated and made to fit in with this principle and with the emotional, inspirational character of all his thought. When it is accepted that economics is a branch of ethics, Martí may be claimed as an economist, not before. If he urged a less bookish and more industrial and agricultural type of education, it was in his own special way, for teachers and county agents were to sow the seed of love and tenderness quite as much as they were to explain new fertilizers and cultivators. He did give a practical attention to forest conservation, the introduction wherever possible of modern industry, better salesmanship of the natural products which Latin America possesses in abundance. Mother earth, he held, in one way or another can of her bounty provide for the independence of the individual, and through him for the greatness of the nation, if we will work hard and avoid the suicidal folly of mono-culture. Laborers are needed in the vineyard, but let them bring their families and some skill and training, or they will prove enemies within the state.

Economics was important to him because without economic justice there can be no liberty for all. The sure road to colonial status is to permit oneself to be seller rather than buyer, and seller to a single customer.

Martí's economic program had a few simple planks: the division of the land, the education of the Indian, the opening of means of communication, dropping useless literary education on the elementary level and substituting a scientific type of training—then sitting back and watching the nation grow.

These practical suggestions have received less attention in the myriad lyrical meditations on Martí than the high-sounding phrases that sing and shout his final goals —liberty, happiness, justice, or the anti-imperialistic patriotism which made him insist that it was better to sink or swim by one's own efforts than to contract a debt of gratitude to a powerful neighbor, and the criticisms he pointed at that neighbor for its failure to solve its own problems of unity and well-being.

Whether his own solutions are not sometimes ingenuous or verbal is a question. It is all very well to agree with the finding of the anthropologists that there are no races and never have been, but to jump from that assertion to the conclusion that there can be no such thing as race hatred seems an exercise in logic rather than in social observation. To solve the population problem with the line, "There are no contradictions in nature; the earth will know how to feed all the men it creates," seems a bit less than adequate. It is perhaps unfair to judge him by single utterances; it is certainly unfair to forget that he grew and changed his ideas, was more individualistic, more the lover of beautifully linked sounds in his romantic and idealistic youth; more scientific, more materialistic, more revolutionary in his attitudes toward capitalism and imperialism and religion, more the tactician of an historic movement in the years after 1887. In the earlier period his reading, and to some extent his friendships, revealed the sentimental and romantic tendency. Later, in North America, we find him supplementing the pomp and circumstance of Victor Hugo with the writings of Spencer and Darwin, Marx and Henry George. He never became the disciple, and never ceased to emphasize spiritual factors in a way that to say the least is not predominant in Marx. He does epitomize the progress of Latin-American thought from enthusiasm for the ideals of the French Revolution, the rights of man, to the ideals of socialism, which he understood to mean an emphasis upon man's duties. His life was given in the struggle for political liberty, but he would believe he had failed utterly if salvation from one tyranny ended in our being delivered over to another, that of a class which exploits those below it in the social order. Only so close does he come to being a precursor of Lenin.

3

JORGE MAÑACH

❋

The Crisis of the Old Culture

The revival of Cuban nationalism in the 1920's was in part a reaction to the spreading influence of North American institutions and ideas. Jorge Mañach and other young intellectuals were convinced that the humanistic elements in Cuban culture were being rapidly eroded by utilitarian and materialistic currents from the United States. In order to reassert what were considered to be authentic Cuban values, Mañach founded the literary magazine *Avance* in 1927. His 1933 biography of José Martí stressed Martí's embodiment of these values and contributed to the elevation of Martí to the status of folk hero of the Cuban nation.

Mañach had a broad education and held degrees in science, law, philosophy, and letters. He was also active in politics, and like numerous other intellectuals of his generation, he became increasingly conservative after the 1930's.

Translated from Jorge Mañach, *La Crisis de la alta cultura en Cuba* (Havana, Sociedad Económica de Amigos del País, 1925), pp. 21–24.

Let us take note, in the first place, of the almost complete lack of disinterested intellectual activity among us, activity which in other countries is indulged in outside of professional activities, not in the fashion of a dilettante, but with rigor, with disciplined zeal, and with the serious ambitions of a second profession. . . . And having imposed these limits, how many examples could you cite of men who . . . steal time in which to dedicate themselves to noble things, as well as to less productive tasks of the study, the laboratory, and the library. You may say that life is very demanding, that appreciation is lacking, the climate is unpropitious, that the necessary material means do not exist. All that is true in part . . . but the fact is that we lack that high and daring force, that spirited and heroic dedication to the loftiest ideal of understanding. The Varonas, the Aramburos, the Ortizes, the Guerras, the Chacón y Calvos—can you not count them on the fingers of one hand?

Aside from that lack of marginal dedication to certain special disciplines, we notice also that the type of learned encyclopedist is disappearing—the type of man well-versed in various branches of knowledge. Our intellectual curiosity . . . has been infected in this way by the urge to specialize implicit in the theories of North American pragmatism. The modern interest in the utilitarian and the practical has grown so extensively among us that we no longer produce the "curious ones" of times past, with whom one could wander in conversation through the most winding and diverse paths of human knowledge. How many men of today have really read Ovid and Goethe, or studied old theologies, or drunk at least in passing in the springs of philosophy? In the old days everyone's great-grandfather was or was not a supporter of Krause, had read his classics and encyclopedias, and waited with excitement for the latest arrival of some rare and abstruse work which the slow sailboats were bringing him from Europe. Today we busy ourselves with little but background articles (without background) and, perhaps, some novel of ambiguous notoriety.

. . .

And if it is true that we are more lacking each day in superior, liberal works and the man of rich culture and erudition, could we not say as much about important investigation in the less disinterested types of knowledge —that is, in those which are more closely related to the improvement of man's daily life? I, gentlemen, . . . want to be and am deeply optimistic but my optimism refers strictly to the future, and I look at the present without indulgence. . . . We have, it is true, in the professional and scientific class men whom we call "illustres." In the legal field . . . we can produce up to a half dozen names endowed with great eminence, the names of wise lawyers who . . . have achieved genuine distinction for themselves and for their country. However, although these men are exceptional, most of them could be justly reproached for not having contributed more to the permanent juridical culture of their country—for example, by collecting in writing the fruit of their knowledge and experience. Within the profession it is clearly noticeable that the old kind of lawyer, deep thinking and erudite, is disappearing, giving way to an avalanche of lawyers with only a very matter-of-fact training, sometimes acquired at a meteor-like speed. The legal profession has deteriorated not only in its moral tone but also in its culture. It no longer produces wise lawyers, only "smart" lawyers.

Though I do not want to condemn fields of which I have no first-hand knowledge, I understand that something very similar . . . is occurring in the other professions. In medicine it is significant that the learned doctor or clinician is giving way to the practical type, the surgeon. In the technical professions like architecture and engineering (where the professional title is already considered unnecessary because the expert mechanic and contractor are enough to satisfy the present demand) a gradual impoverishment of great skill, good taste and the will to innovate is becoming evident.

In other professions more removed from the utilitarian demands, the lack of stimuli to superior learning is making the enthusiasm and spontaneous desire to excel and to perfect oneself rare. This is happening in teaching where the old Cuban teachers, spiritual mentors of generations like Father Varela and don José de la Luz, are no longer emulated. The decadence of the university classroom, on the other hand, has lately become so notorious a phenomenon . . . that it would hardly need stressing, were our present cultural poverty not due to this more than to any other single influence.

4

DUVON C. CORBITT

❋

Cuban Revisionist Interpretations of Cuba's Struggle for Independence

---

Until quite recently very few North American historians devoted their efforts to Cuban history. Duvon C. Corbitt is one of the most active of this small group. For a number of years he taught at Candler College in Havana, and his consistent devotion to Cuban studies led to works covering various facets of the island's past. His close association with many Cuban historians uniquely qualifies him to analyze the relationship between historiography and the nationalistic feelings of Cuban intellectuals. Professor Corbitt is currently on the faculty of Asbury College in Wilmore, Kentucky.

From Duvon C. Corbitt, "Cuban Revisionist Interpretations of Cuba's Struggle for Independence," *Hispanic American Historical Review,* XLIII (August, 1963), 395–400, 402–403. Reprinted by permission of the Duke University Press and of the author.

As late as 1927 history texts in use in Cuban schools were still presenting the island's struggles for independence in much the same manner as they were treated in history textbooks in this country; that is, (1) early plots, conspiracies, and attempts at invasion down to about 1865 which aimed at cutting Cuba loose from Spain (often thought of as aiming at annexation to the United States); (2) the reformist movement of the late Fifties and Sixties when Cubans hoped for freedom within the Spanish connection; (3) the failure of the reformist efforts followed by the first war for independence, known as the Ten Years' War, 1868–78; (4) the Guerra Chiquita of 1878–80 led by Cuban generals who refused to accept the Peace of Zanjón; (5) the autonomist movement once more aiming at liberty within the Spanish Empire; (6) its failure followed by the War for Independence, 1895–98; and, finally, La Guerra Hispanoamericana in 1898 (Cuban texts still used the Spanish version of "Spanish-American War," which term has since become anathema to Cuban historians as well as politicians).

Most school texts as well as larger histories had good words for the administration of General Leonard Wood during the First Intervention (1899–1902), saying little about his predecessor in that position, General John R. Brooke. There were expressions of regret and even resentment over the failure of the United States government to recognize the government of the "República en Armas" which had directed Cuban efforts in the War for Independence, but for the most part, criticism of this policy was soft-pedaled, censure being reserved for the imposition of the Platt Amendment and later interventions and meddling in Cuban affairs under the Amendment. Charles E. Magoon, the United States governor during the Second Intervention, was a favorite target, charged with having, by precept and example, instructed Cuban politicians in the ways of graft and other forms of corruption.

This is not to insinuate that historical revisionism had no advocates among the scholars of the island. From 1910 the Academy of History (organized after the models of those of France and Spain) was a center through which such intellects as Fernando Ortiz, Enrique José Varona, Raimundo Cabrera, Rafael Fernandez de Castro, José Miró Argentier, Juan Miguel Dihigo, Enrique Collazo, Francisco de Paula Coronado, Tomás Justiz, Emeterio S. Santovenia, and Carlos M. Trelles, promoted investigation. Since most of them had been participants in one or more phases of the independence efforts, it is understandable that their historical work was directed in great part toward clarifying and interpreting the events that had led to the separation from Spain and the establishment of the Republic. Much of what they did was necessarily revisionist in nature, but was carried out in the best tradition of scientific historians who seek the facts and present them with as little conscious bias as possible.

More nearly revisionist in the early years of the Republic was a group that gathered around Dr. Fernando Ortiz, long time member of the Academy of History and for a while its president. Primarily interested in problems of sociology, anthropology, archeology, and folklore, Dr. Ortiz, nevertheless formed a nucleus for younger scholars to whom he lent inspiration. Once a week they lunched together and exchanged intellectual findings. One of the number later characterized the members of this circle as *inconformes*. The writer had the pleasure of attending one of these *almuerzos* in December of 1959.

The member of the inconformes who is perhaps best known of any of the revisionists in this country is Herminio Portell Vilá, who has refused to become fixed in any one school and has remained pretty much of a free lance as a historical writer as he has in politics, journalism, and radio and television newscasting. As a result he has often been dubbed anti-United States in this country and pro-United States in his own.

In 1930 Dr. Portell Vilá published the first of his three volume definitive study on *Narciso López y su época.* Although the other two volumes did not appear until 1952 and 1959 respectively, the first was sufficient to make clear the author's thesis (announced two years earlier in his history of his home town of Cárdenas) that López was an advocate of complete independence for Cuba and not of annexation to the United States. This volume also gave its author a high rating, both in and out of Cuba, as a careful, painstaking investigator and able writer, and paved the way for a Guggenheim fellowship that enabled him to continue his studies during his exile from the Machado dictatorship which came close upon the heels of this publication. This opportunity he used (with the coöperation of his wife) to explore archives and other sources in the United States for material on the whole story of the relations between this country and Cuba, as well as to gather further data on López. The result is perhaps the most thorough piece of revisionist historical writing yet to come from a Cuban —the four volume *Historia de Cuba en sus relaciones con los Estados Unidos y España.*

. . .

Considerably before Dr. Portell Vilá achieved prominence as a historian, the man who was destined to become the center around which the revisionists were to gather, had already made a name for himself in a number of fields of writing. In 1912, at the age of 23, Emilio Roig de Leuchsenring of Habana won first prize in a *costumbrista* contest with his near classic *Se puede vivir en la Habana sin un centavo?* His later writings on the history of Havana and Cuban folklore are among the best on the subjects. But without losing interest in his first love, Dr. Roig turned more and more to broader topics of history, including the impact of United States influence in Cuban affairs. In 1922 he published a volume entitled *La enmienda Platt, su interpretación primitiva y sus aplicaciones posteriores hasta 1921,* followed the next year by his *Análisis y consecuencias de la intervención norteamericana en los asuntos interiores de Cuba.* Two years later came his pamphlet with the significant title, *La colonia superviva. Cuba a los veintidós años de la República,* the contents of which foreshadowed later assertions by the same author and other revisionists that Cuba's battle for independence did not end in 1898, nor even in 1902, but that in later years it only entered into another phase with the United States as the enemy of Cuban independence instead of Spain.

It was in 1927 that Dr. Roig first entered the field that was to make it possible for him to assume dynamic leadership of most of Cuba's revisionist historians. In that year the mayor of Havana placed him in charge of historical studies of the city with the title of *comisionado municipal,* which position he used to promote a series of studies in the city's archives on Havana under Spain. Radical changes in Havana's administration by the dictator Machado forced Dr. Roig from this position in 1931 and eventually into exile, but after Machado's fall in 1933 he returned to the city hall with the new title of Historiador de la Ciudad de la Habana, which he held continuously until the present upheaval, and which office he organized and expanded into a center of historical investigation and interpretation that has rivaled the Academy of History, although that was not his original intention, for Dr. Roig was one of the inner circle of the Academy until he resigned from it in the late Thirties.

He had scarcely taken possession of the Office of City Historian when from it he launched a series of historical conferences, adult education courses on historical exposition open to the public, and sponsored several series of historical publications including one of the colonial records of the municipality under the title *Actas Capitulares del Ayuntamiento de la Habana,* the *Colección Histórica Cubana y Americana,* and the more popular *Cuadernos de Historia Habanera.* By 1959 more than one hundred volumes of historical studies had been published by the Oficina del Historiador de la Ciudad de la Habana.

To such a center historically minded persons naturally gravitated. In 1940, in conjunction with a number of them, Dr. Roig launched the Sociedad Cubana de Estudios Históricos e Internacionales, broadly based so as to admit all those interested in historical studies—for he and many others thought of the Academy as too exclusive, and too conservative. Two years later this society and the office of the City Historian joined in promoting the First National Historical Congress of Cuba, the Thirteenth of which met in February of 1960. It was intended that the Congresses should be annual affairs, and they were until 1952, after which the political situation under Dictator Batista became impropitious for such meetings since they were invariably forums for some very plain-spoken opinions on such matters as dictatorship, imperialism, and colonialism. The papers presented to these historical congresses, the addresses actually delivered, and especially the resolutions and recommendations approved, are among the best sources of information on the revisionist interpretations of Cuban history.

The papers and discussions at the first such congress (1942) covered a wide variety of subjects on the history of all of the Americas as well as that of Cuba itself. Those touching on Cuban independence movements were only mildly revisionist—with one exception, that written by Dr. Roig himself, entitled *Revaloración de la Guerra Libertadora Cubana de 1895*. This did not appear in the published report of the congress, but was left for separate printing. Actually Dr. Roig used it as a stepping stone to a number of studies on the whole independence movement which have set the tone for the revisionists. The most significant of these works are: *La Guerra Libertadora Cubana de los Treinta Años, 1868–98; La lucha cubana por la república, contra la anexión y la Enmienda Platt, 1899–1902; Juan Gualberto Gómez, paladín de la independencia de Cuba;* and *La Guerra Hispano-Cubano-*

americana fue ganado por el Lugarteniente General del Ejército Libertador Calixto García Iñiguez (all from the Oficina del Historiador de la Ciudad de la Habana, the first two in 1952 and the others in 1954 and 1955 respectively). In all of them Dr. Roig insisted that the struggle for independence was not a series of wars but one continuous struggle of thirty years' duration; that there were never lacking in the United States friends of Cuban freedom, but that our government was consistently opposed to Cuban independence. He further insisted that the entry of the United States into the struggle in 1898 was not necessary for Cuban victory, because the Cuban patriots had the mother country defeated by that time; furthermore, after entering the war the United States found it necessary to use Cuban plans of strategy and Cuban forces to win the Santiago campaign; that Spanish defeat did not bring Cuban freedom but simply turned the struggle into a new phase with the United States as the opponent.

Much of this had been foreshadowed in Dr. Roig's publications of 1921-22, and 1924, already cited. In these later works he documented heavily his statements about the incapacity of General Shafter, his discourtesy to Calixto García and to other Cuban officers during the Santiago campaign, and particularly about Shafter's refusal to permit García to share in the surrender negotiations or in the surrender ceremonies, after having used his battle plans, his leadership, and his army to achieve victory. Objection was made to the name, "The Spanish-American War" because the Cubans were given no credit. As opposed to this the revisionists for their part suggested a variety of more acceptable names, finally obtaining from the Cuban Congress a law officially adopting that of "Guerra Hispano-Cubanoamericana." The revisionists assert that the war was won before the United States entered and robbed them of the fruits of victory.

Dr. Roig, along with others of his persuasion, praises Senator Teller for insisting that the United States announce to the world a guarantee that it was entering the Cuban struggle to obtain freedom for the island instead of to annex it. They also praise General John R. Brooke, the first governor under the Intervention, for his efforts in behalf of Cuban independence, but severely condemn Elihu Root, President McKinley, Leonard Wood, and Theodore Roosevelt as rabid imperialists seeking to annex the island. . . .

. . .

While the most conservative historians in Cuba agreed with a number of these assertions, there have not been lacking scholars who rejected them in whole or in part. Noteworthy are two works by "The Grand Old Man" of Cuban history and diplomacy, Cosme de la Torriente. In his *Fin de la dominación de España en Cuba* and *Calixto García cooperó con las fuerzas armadas de los Estados Unidos en 1898, cumpliendo órdenes del gobierno cubano,* Torriente admitted the crudity of Shafter, but contended that this did not represent the studied policy of the United States or its leaders, pointing out the effort of General Nelson A. Miles to make amends. Torriente also expressed doubts (and he was García's chief of staff) about the ability of the Cuban army to defeat the Spanish forces without the assistance of the United States navy. This view is also expressed in a paper read before the Cuban Academy of History by Julio Morales Coello, entitled *La importancia del poderío naval—positivo y negativo—en el desarrollo y en la independencia de Cuba.*

Much the same conservative line was followed in the ten volume *Historia de la Nación Cubana,* prepared in commemoration of the fiftieth anniversary of the Republic. This was a coöperative effort of many scholars, drawn in great part from the Academy group. Nearly all of these writers are well known in Hispanic American circles in this country. The directors of the project were Emeterio S. Santovenia, Ramiro Guerra, Juan J. Remos, and José María Pérez Cabrera. While the list of contributors contained such revisionists' names as Enrique Gay-Calbó, Julio Le Riverend, and other collaborators with Dr. Roig in the work of the Sociedad Cubana de Estudios Cubanos e Internacionales, the majority leaned more toward the conservative school. In dealing with United States' participation in the Cuban independence movements, Dr. Remos contributed a section under the traditional title "La Guerra Hispano-Americana," already condemned as heretical and anti-patriotic by the revisionists; in fact, it was technically illegal since the Cuban Congress had passed a law in May of 1945 (in conformity with a recommendation from the Historical Congresses in question) making official the name "La Guerra Hispano-Cubanoamericana."

I myself heard caustic criticism of the editorial policy of the directors of the *Historia de la Nación Cubana* and their sponsors, largely on account of their conservatism and traditionalism, and because the Cuban government of the hour contributed to the costs of publication and was suspected of dictating the tone. This is highly improbable for the scholars who produced this history were (and are) among the best prepared, the most objective, and the most scientific historians of Cuba, comparable in ability to the best in any country in the world; in fact, their objectivity and their inclination toward conservatism were two of their strong points, but the revisionists were neither in a conservative nor an objective mood. They had been impatiently striving for a generation to correct what they considered false interpretations of their country's history. While the traditionalists were accepted in this country both in historical and diplomatic circles, the revisionists were often frowned upon, even to the extent of being considered communists.

5

EMILIO ROIG DE LEUCHSENRING

❋

A Cuban Historian's View of the Struggle for Independence

Emilio Roig de Leuchsenring was one of the most productive and controversial historians in twentieth-century Cuba. Beginning his career shortly after 1900, he published books until his death in 1964. Professor Roig consistently opposed the power and influence of the United States, concentrating on correcting what he considered the errors in North American views of Cuban history. As one of the leaders of the "revisionist" school of Cuban historians, he was instrumental in forming the Cuban Society of Historical and International Studies and in the campaign to change the name of the 1898 War to the Spanish-Cuban-American War. He also worked diligently to emphasize the role played by Cubans in the struggle which freed the island from Spanish rule, a struggle which he titled the Thirty Years War.

Translated from Emilio Roig de Leuchsenring, *Cuba no debe su Independencia a los Estados Unidos,* 3rd ed. (Havana, Edicíones La Tertulia, 1960), pp. 11–14, 153–155.

Professor Roig served for many years as Historian of the City of Havana. In this capacity he promoted the publication of many volumes on Cuban history. Through his writing and other activities Professor Roig played an important role in the development of those historical concepts which helped shape the intellectual content of the Castro Revolution.

Unlike some nations, the Cuban nation was not brought into being at the end of a serious world conflict by the agreements or intrigues of great powers who drew nations on the map at the international conference table. Neither is Cuba an agglutination of regions complicated by racial, religious, or political heterogeneity; nor does it owe its existence to the self-interest of other nations. (If such help had been necessary, Cuba would never have become part of the international community of nations.)

To the contrary, the Cuban nation is the result of a long evolutionary process involving the thought and action of sons of this land in their search for political guides which would resolve immediately and permanently the many problems which confronted our people in various epochs during the colonial period. This was the process of molding Cuban consciousness to provide for the integration of national sentiment.

. . .

As in the case of the North American colonies, freedom from colonial despotism was the goal of this development of the nationalistic idea: the great revolutionary political movement for independence whose prologue was the rebellion for economic liberty launched by *vegueros* [tobacco growers] in 1717 against Spanish imperialism, and repeated in 1723. The liberation movement originated with the first conspiracy of Román de la Luz, Luis F. Basabe, and Joaquín Infante (which was discovered and aborted in 1810), and culminated in 1898. During this time we should not forget the uprising for racial liberty led by José Antonio Aponte in 1812, nor the fierce repression of the slave uprising of 1844, called *La Escalera* [the ladder]. For a period of two centuries, a host of conspiracies and expeditions were watered with the blood of the protomartyrs of our liberty. In this struggle black and white Cubans . . . united in the pursuit of a common ideal. They set forth in the sole hope of breaking all ties with Spain, having been convinced that it was useless to make peaceful demands for improvements and reforms, justice and liberty.

. . .

As the revolutionary assembly of Jimaguayú declared on September 16, 1895, . . . the war which began on February 24 of that year was a continuation of the war which started on October 10, 1868, and that the Cuban people on the island and in exile had carried on this struggle during the intervening period. . . . This is what authorized Lieutenant General of the Liberating Army, Calixto García Iñiquez, to say in his letter of protest to Major General W. R. Shafter (the head of the North American forces in the Spanish-Cuban-American War of 1898) that the Cuban right to participate in the capitulation and delivery by the Spaniards of the city of Santiago de Cuba had been negated, and that the war which ended with this surrender was "a thirty year struggle against Spanish domination."

. . .

Cuba does not owe its independence to the United States of America, but only to the efforts of its own people in their firm, irrevocable will to end the injustices, abuses, discriminations, and exploitations which took place under the despotic colonial regime, and to gain liberty, democracy, justice, culture and civilization. . . .

. . .

The North American state was always the enemy of Cuban independence. It obstructed or annulled the efforts of the Cuban patriots in their attempts to send to the island expeditions with materials of war and medicines. It stubbornly resisted recognizing a state of war. On the other hand, at various times it offered material support to Spain in order to keep the island under its domination, even volunteering to help recover it if the island were lost by Spain. This was in evident contrast to the sympathies for the cause of Cuban liberty demonstrated by the North American people, who promptly decided to co-operate with the efforts of the revolutionaries in the U.S. Many of these citizens participated in the military struggle and some of them gave their lives for Free Cuba.

In 1898 national opinion in the United States not only favored the right of the Cubans to liberty and independence, but also official recognition of the Republic constituted in the camp of the armed forces. The North American government betrayed the people's will when the recognition which had been accorded by the Senate was suppressed in the Joint Resolution voted by Congress on April 18, 1898, and signed by the president on the 20th.

6

CHARLES JOHNSON POST

The Cuban Soldier and the War for Independence: A North American View

---

North American males flocked to the colors in 1898 to participate in a "crusade" to free Cuba. Very quickly, however, the emphasis on "Cuba libre" began to vanish and the people of the United States were informed that the Cubans were a lazy, cowardly sort who were obviously unable to govern themselves. Poor reporting was one reason for this new emphasis, but desire to sell the gospel of empire was also involved. "The taste of empire is in the mouth of the people even as the taste of blood in the jungle," editorialized the *Washington Post*, and in the process of acquiring this appetite the heroic struggles of the Cuban revolutionaries were all but forgotten.

Charles Johnson Post was an exception. He

From Charles Johnson Post, *The Little War of Private Post* (New York, Little, Brown, 1961), pp. 91–94. Copyright © 1960, by Alice L. Post and Phyllis Bradford Post. Reprinted by permission of Little, Brown and Co.

served in the infantry of the United States Army during the war with Spain and developed there an appreciation for the ability of the Cuban soldiers. Post's lack of racial prejudice was basic to his willingness to accept Cubans on the basis of equality and respect. Unfortunately, the racist attitude of many of his fellow countrymen contributed to the problems of U.S.–Cuban relations.

Post was an artist and writer whose work appeared in various leading periodicals and newspapers. He worked in Latin America for several years, and his last position was that of Commissioner of Conciliation with the Department of Labor.

Cuban troops kept arriving from scattered points throughout the Santiago Province. We all traded with the ragged insurgents. Their rebel battalions looked with awe on our vast resources of food. We found a ready market for trade in our sowbelly or canned corned beef or hardtack. They had mangoes, the sweet, rather turpentinish flavor of which fascinated us. And they had platanos, a fruit that looks like huge, green bananas with coarse skin. The platano is an acquired taste—and we never acquired it.

For haversacks, the ragged insurgents had jute sugar sacks or, in better cases, Pillsbury's flour sacks. There were always platanos in them and a few sticks of sugar cane. As mess cups the Cubans used half a coconut shell; and often their canteen was an old cognac bottle. We traded for the sugar cane, and learned to shave off slivers of it and chew them instead of, as at first, trying to gnaw on the whole stalk.

The war correspondents sneered at these Cubans and ridiculed their rags, their rifles, and their fighting! The correspondents knew nothing of it. Some years later I met and became acquainted with General Frederick

Funston, who was with them, shoulder-to-shoulder, as chief of their artillery before the United States entered the Cuban revolution after the sinking of the Maine. Their revolution had to be fought with guerrilla tactics; there was no quarter on either side. Jungle hospitals were massacred; and only in the cities and fortified towns were the Spaniards safe. No troops ever received warmer praise than that which came from General Funston for these tattered troops with their varied rifles and scanty ammunition. Barefoot, or only in rawhide sandals, they could outmarch any of the professional armies. I have seen them, and side by side with our column when they had to make time. They swung along in single file over the narrow trail, in an easy stride that had the suggestion of a lope in it. When they came to a shallow brook, they splashed through it. Some, thirsty, fell out of the column and knelt to drink their fill. Others shuffled on through without losing their place in the column, and as they moved they scooped up water and lapped it from their cupped hands.

General Funston knew their courage, their heroism, their stoicism, and their idealism. He was one of that growing group who understood our Latin neighbors, who knew them as fighting men and soldiers. Cubans, perhaps, know us better than we know them. It should be mutual. For the Cubans in their series of rebellions for freedom from Spain had much in common, in the campaigns and in their aspirations, with our own soldiers of the American Revolution against the fattish autocracy of King George. They had Calixto García and Maceo, and scores like them. We have only to recall the days and the troops of Marion, the Swamp Fox of the Carolinas, to be able to picture those *insurrectos* in the province of Santa Clara and its village.

. . .

All day the Cuban troops came marching in. Their officers were mounted on what were little more than scrawny ponies; and it was difficult to tell an officer from a private in that army. For months they had been out on guerrilla warfare, laying ambuscades and avoiding pitched battles. Used to the hill trails, or to no trails, they came in a column of twos, and each man carried his rifle as best suited him.

These Cubans were a curiosity to us. We spoke no Spanish, and they no English. But, when we gathered with them, they would rub their stomachs and say "Hambre." And this means "What have you got to eat?" in any language.

Their uniform was but a jacket and breeches; the jacket ragged and in some cases a mere lacework of tatters. Each carried a machete and one or two cartridge bandoliers of denim or sacking. Over his shoulder was a gunny sack or canvas hammock, in which he carried, among other things, his rawhide sandals, or the fiber-soled *alpagatas,* for when the going was easy he went barefoot. Some wore hats, the straw Cuban sombrero, but rain-soaked and shapeless. Here and there in their column would be a commissary mule straddled with two huge baskets or bags, holding the heavier supplies of the regiment and its officers, including a few iron pots; the rest of the space was filled with platanos and bundles of sugar cane.

There was no ammunition train; there was no ammunition except that which each man carried. And there were empty bandoliers in that column too. Those with full bandoliers generally carried a Spanish Mauser rifle—a sign of valor in action; it meant a dead Spaniard —but most of the Cubans were armed with Remingtons and Winchesters.

Duty in the little chains of outlying blockhouses was definitely disliked by the Spanish troops, for the jungle was all about them from the edge of the little vegetable garden which each blockhouse tended. And beyond the edge some Cuban scout might be lying in ambush. If the Spaniard was unarmed, as a precaution against losing his Mauser, he lost his life in a machete stroke. Pursuit in these jungles or their trails was dangerous. The insurrectos often tried to bait the Spaniards into pursuing them—and running into an ambuscade. The blockhouses dotted all of Cuba; they were within range of each other, and technically in support, but in fact they became little isolated garrisons patiently waiting their turn for relief.

The Mausers the insurrectos captured were excellent weapons, but there was no ammunition for them—beyond the beltfull unbuckled from a dead Spaniard. Ammunition was precious. Never was there enough in any rebel command to fight a pitched battle, even if that had been good strategy. Curiously, it was Havana—stronghold and main citadel of the Spanish commander in chief, General Weyler—that became the chief source of the insurrecto's supply of Mauser cartridges.

It was the prostitutes of Havana and other cities who supplied the rebels, as I learned later from my friend Alfredo Poey.

From an ordinary private soldier of the Spanish Army, *soldado raso,* they would demand 100 Mauser cartridges. From a noncommissioned officer, the demand would be for 200 cartridges or more. With an officer the demand rose steeply—a box of 1,000 cartridges. It was, said Poey, an amiable arrangement all round. The Spanish soldier's pay was small and luxuries were expensive. But cartridges—*Mira, hombre!* They are the issue of the government, they cost nothing, *Vámanos!*

At night a friend of the prostitute would call. He had a load of wood or charcoal or sugar cane, or some wine. When he left, his saddle pads would be lined with Mauser bullets. Thus the insurrectos kept themselves supplied with a frugal ammunition. For their artillery, and for rifles other than the Mauser, they depended upon the gunrunning little steamers or the fishing boats that, every now and again, were caught by the Spanish patrol boats fringing the Cuban coast. I have no doubt that various of the Mauser cartridges I saw in Cuban bandoliers had come through the underground by way of Havana's ladies of the night.

7

CHESTER LLOYD JONES

A North American View of the Relationship of Modern Cuba to the Policies and Interests of the United States

---

The United States has played an important role in the history of modern Cuba. It is impossible to understand United States policies without knowing the attitudes and ideas behind them. The following selection is representative of what might be called the standard interpretation. It is a combination of strategic, economic, and cultural elements which emphasizes the prime importance of order and stability as defined by a creditor nation. As the Commercial Attaché in Cuba in 1921, Chester

---

From Chester Lloyd Jones, *Caribbean Interests of the United States* (New York, D. Appleton and Co., 1919), pp. 80–81, 83–88.

Lloyd Jones, wrote: "Capital investment should be encouraged in Cuba to a greater extent than in other foreign countries, because . . . it is easier to guarantee the protection of the rights of the investors than is the case in other countries."

Jones served the State Department in various capacities, and wrote several volumes on U.S.–Caribbean relations. He also taught political science at the University of Wisconsin.

Pre-eminent among the islands of the Caribbean is Cuba. The most prized of the Spanish possessions after the revolt of the colonies in South and Central America, it became an independent republic as a result of the treaty of peace of December 10, 1898, at the end of the Spanish-American War. Since then, in spite of local disturbances, it has risen to a position relatively much more important in the Caribbean than it ever held under the Spanish régime. The advance which has come is due not only to the natural resources of the country, but also to the peculiar political arrangements entered into only half willingly by the local government.

During the negotiation of the treaty of peace, Spain had expressed her fear that left to itself the island might become Africanized. The examples of the Dominican Republic and Haiti aroused fears that Cuba independent might be a prey to frequent revolutions with the result that neither property nor personal rights would be protected. To save the island from the consequences of a "premature" independence, Spain wished to have the United States keep at least a degree of control sufficient to insure order. No express engagement on this point appears in the treaty. The property rights of residents of Cuba, it was declared, would not be impaired and the United States, so long as its occupation lasted, undertook "to assume and discharge the obligations that may, under international law, result from the fact of its occupation for the protection of life and property."

The subsequent action of the United States showed, however, that there was no intent on its part to allow international complications to arise through a disturbance of local order in the island. . . .

. . .

Whether the Cuban people possess or can develop the degree of self-control necessary for self-government is still, in view of recent history, an open question. Extravagance in expenditure and willingness to consider the holding of public office as an opportunity for taking selfish advantages, rather than as a call to service, have been far too prominent characteristics of Cuban politics. Disputes over the patronage have been incessant; the public debt has risen constantly. Starting practically debt free, the public obligations reached $62,083,100, in 1911, before the end of a decade of local control. In 1914, the total was $67,620,000. This does not represent a burdensome debt. With the rapidly increasing economic strength of the island it can be easily borne. But the purposes for which the debt was created are significant. Judged by the actual return to the people, which was made possible by the loans, there appears to be still considerable doubt whether Cuba will be able to prove herself beyond the need of guidance by stronger powers in financial affairs.

Even considered apart from the general Caribbean situation, Cuba is important to the United States, not only because of this responsibility assumed to assure public order in the island. There are with the "Pearl of the Antilles," in addition, important military and commercial connections.

The operations of the Spanish-American War had again demonstrated what long had been evident to those at all familiar with our naval affairs—the desirability of acquiring for the United States at least one naval base in the West Indies. . . .

. . .

. . . These settlements are of great importance in that, now in possession of Porto Rico and with a strong naval base in Cuba, the United States is in an exceptionally advantageous position to carry out the obligations it has assumed for the preservation of order in the Caribbean, and occupies a commanding position on the trade routes which pass to the Panama Canal.

Both in the United States and Cuba there has developed a desire to bind the two countries closely together in their trade relations. Commercially, the island is naturally dependent upon its northern neighbor. That its products did not seek our ports in much greater quantities even before the island secured its independence was due only to the tariff policy of Spain. The investments of our citizens in Cuba and the commerce which had been built up with the island in the later years of Spanish control were influences which increased American interest in the island's struggle for independence. . . .

. . .

. . . Like Porto Rico, but unlike other Caribbean divisions, the population is largely of white blood. The census of 1907 reported 1,428,176, or 69.7 percent, of the population as white, while the negroes number 274,272, mixed 334,695, and Chinese 11,837. Among the whites there were 203,637 foreign born, of whom 185,393 were Spanish and 6,713 from the United States. From such a community much may be expected. Though the climate may limit the sort of labor that may be secured, this is not, like Jamaica or Haiti, a black man's country. The racial composition of the population as between white and black compares favorably with that of some of the southern commonwealths of the United States. The proportion of non-white blood is about the same as in North Carolina and much less than in Alabama, Florida, Georgia, Louisiana or Mississippi. The white element in Cuba and in the southern United States is itself, of course, of radically different stock, but the performance of the Cuban people in the last decade and a half shows characteristics which, so far as economic advance is concerned, are decidedly encouraging. There is no more heartening evidence of what the Spanish-American can do in a semitropical climate than that offered by Cuba.

It is when we turn to the figures of recent trade development that the importance of Cuba is impressed upon us most vividly. In 1896, the year after the insurrection against the mother country broke out, our exchanges already reached a value of over forty-seven and a half million dollars. In 1898, the year of the war, they fell to less than twenty-five million. Thereafter, both imports and exports grew steadily; in 1901, they totaled over $69,000,000. After the commercial treaty of 1903 an even greater portion of the foreign trade sought and came from United States ports. It was valued at over $120,000,000 in 1908, and at over $182,000,000 in spite of local disturbances in 1912. In 1914, it reached $200,188,222.

. . .

Cuba thus ranked fifth among all countries from which the United States imported goods and took sixth place among her customers. Cuban trade with the United States amounted to twice that with Belgium, to almost four times that with Spain or with Russia in Europe, to almost eight times that with Sweden. Compared to other Caribbean regions this trade total makes the importance of Cuba even more striking. Cuba's trade with the United States is about seven times as great as that of the Central American states and thirteen times as great as that of Haiti and the Dominican Republic, in spite of the dominant position the country holds in the markets of these regions.

The greatest increase in the economic importance of Cuba has come recently. Only Mexico has shown a comparable advance. The chief causes of the change have been the establishment of greater security for property following the Spanish-American War and the resulting increase in the investments of foreign capital.

8

HERMINIO PORTELL VILÁ

The Nationalism of the Cuban Intellectuals

In the 1920's, nationalistic sentiment in Cuba became increasingly vigorous and articulate. The young intellectuals were among the most active proponents of this new nationalism which emphasized reform and opposition to the influence of the United States. Herminio Portell Vilá is a good example of this generation and his many scholarly works reflect its hopes and feelings. In the late 1930's he published his four-volume work on the history of Cuba in its relations with Spain and the United States; the following selection is taken from the introduction. In these volumes Professor Portell Vilá presents a stirring defense of Cuba's right to be a sovereign nation and a detailed analysis of the island's struggles against Spanish colonialism and North American annexationism.

In addition to his scholarly activities, Professor Portell Vilá is also an outspoken critic of authori-

---

Translated from Herminio Portell Vilá, *Historia de Cuba en sus Relaciones con los Estados Unidos y España* (Havana, Jesús Montero, 1938), I, 10–14.

tarian government, and has twice chosen exile rather than submission (1930 and 1960).

The importance of our topic hardly needs to be emphasized to the reader; it is the history of a small, insular nation whose independent existence is one of the miracles of modern times. In the conflict of ambitions which raged for several centuries over the possession of Cuba and which involved Spain, the U.S., France and England, Russia, and Prussia, we can also find Mexico, Gran Colombia and Haiti as countries desirous of acquiring Cuba even at the price of a war. Nor did they disdain intrigue, purchase contract, economic influence, etc., as means to that end.

Cuba was for centuries the dangerous topic of international relations. And only through war and ruin did Cuba, with the termination of Spanish sovereignty, finally cease to be the difficult problem of European-American relations. No country of the same size has been so discussed and so coveted in modern times.

Ripped apart by bloody wars of independence just as she was previously blockaded and invaded; used as a battlefield for Spain and her enemies up to 1898; exploited and badly governed; flooded with slaves and with agents of despotism; overwhelmed by a ruinous, colonial economy which ought to have made progress impossible —Cuba has survived all her crises and has advanced greatly in every sphere, most especially since the establishment of the republic.

Whoever has read the history of Cuba in the turbulent pages of international diplomacy and the reprehensible chapters of the colonial epoch can be no less than amazed at the strength demonstrated by the Cuban people. This nation, like every other, has defects, though less than it might, if we keep in mind its antecedents. But it has the outstanding virtues of laboriousness, perseverance, progressive spirit and patriotic feeling. How else can one explain the fact that it endures and that it has progressed?

The material progress of the Cuban nation surpasses that of almost all American nations. It also surpasses most of them in erudition, which it has demonstrated splendidly in little more than thirty years of life as a republic.

For certain simple-minded souls, the explanation of that general progress is none other than close relations with the United States and the formidable example and stimulus of its civilization. I would certainly not deny that real and fertile influence; but it does not tell the whole story, as we will see when we make a detailed analysis of the actual situation. At the present time, it is evident to one who knows the different regions of North America well—not only New York, California, Pennsylvania, New England and certain Midwestern states—that Cuba is more advanced, materially and culturally, than many Southern and Western American states which are near the centers of culture in that country and which have closer relations with them than Cuba does. Therefore, if the theory of North American influence as uniquely responsible for Cuban progress were true, it should be even more applicable in the backward regions of the United States itself.

In both equations all the terms are equal except those two which surely explain why the comparison is surprisingly favorable to Cuba. These two are the Cuban people and the more integrated democracy of Cuba. In the South of the United States, an established oligarchy governs under the fiction of democracy and without responsibility. Under this oligarchy there is hardly any means of livelihood, civil rights, nor any progress for the "sharecroppers," the "poor whites," the "white trash," and the "niggers."

The nation which progresses in spite of the mistakes and the despotism of its mother country; which is always opposed to annexation by neighbors that coveted it—the U.S., Mexico, Gran Colombia and Haiti—and to acquisition by European powers; the nation which before any other in Latin America, before its own mother country, and many other nations in Europe, had railroads, telegraph, steamships, telephone, etc., and which, notwithstanding a parasitic minority, has always been and is hard-working and enterprising, is the one which has made sure that the thirty-five years of the republic—those stormy, difficult and disoriented years of every free country, including the U.S.—have been in Cuba years of continuous progress. Yet this is still not all that the Cubans would have liked to have accomplished.

This small nation, imprisoned on an island, unindustrialized, encountering the indifference if not the hostility of its neighbors, maintained year after year the most gallant struggle for its political emancipation which the annals of the wars of independence in the New World record. It is an incontrovertible fact, revealed by a dispassionate study of American revolutions, that in proportion to the population and the resources, and at times in absolute terms, Cuba put up a greater, more heroic struggle against all the Spanish forces concentrated in only one very small country than did all the other countries of America. And it did so without the aid of French and Spanish expeditionary forces, as in the case of the United States; or without Argentinian support, as in Chile and Peru; or without the kind of help the Colombians gave to the countries liberated by Bolívar.

When the United States intervened in the war between Spain and Cuba, the struggle had been going on for decades. There were battles quite comparable to Bunker Hill, Princeton, Trenton, Chacabuco, Maipú, Pichincha, etc. That similarity is even greater if we compare the efforts of the Cubans with the so-called battles between the Spaniards and North Americans (helped by Cubans) near Santiago de Cuba.

No Cuban, no matter how exaggerated his enthusiasms may be, nor how inactive his nationalistic fervor, can conclude such a study based on truth and just appreciation for norms, without feeling proud of being a Cuban, of belonging to a virile, progressive, industrious nation, a nation enamored of perfection. . . . He must be proud of [a nation] which, because it loves perfection, falls at times into despair, criticizing bitterly—and as if they were national, which they are not—those shortcomings which are results of the process of national integration and the consequences of the colonial past. For this reason their eradication will be easier for Cuba than for other nations.

From what I have said it is evident that my thesis hopes to prove that the history of Cuba is worthy, stimulating, exemplary, and sufficient to support the future of a country admirably equipped for a happy, rich, free, and respectable life.

These days it is claimed that much of the social, economic, and political topsy-turviness of the postwar [era] in Europe is the result of the humiliations, plunder, and violation of the rights of certain nations which are today captives of ruinous, aggressive, despotic totalitarian regimes. Postwar Europe reflects the despair, defeatism, and impotence of the people before foreign abuses. If that argument is worth anything, then in order to bring out the virtues of the Cuban nation and the normalcy of her reactions, let the argument be applied to the case of Cuba, and not a few of the problems of Cuban life during the last forty years will be explained.

The Cuban revolution of 1868–1898 accomplished its goals of destroying the bases of the political, economic, and social structure of the country, in order to reconstruct them to the national advantage. The incendiary torch, the struggle, the reconcentration camps, the defeat of the Spanish party, were preparing the future for a new Cuba when North American intervention re-established and consolidated the economic and social aspects of the destroyed regime, with all their political implications. The liquidation of that North American action has weighed like a very heavy load on the republican life of Cuba, which up to now has been little able to free itself from it.

The frustration of the Cuban revolution—of its formidable effort and its awakened national conscience striving to make a truly new state—was the work of the United States, dictated by those with an appetite for annexation. No nation has been so victimized without [developing] a deep resentment in its resistance to the aggressor, a resentment which permeates the organization of its society and its very life. The fact that the Cubans, frustrated in their hopes and sacrifices, overcame similar discouragements without succumbing to defeatism, is conclusive proof of their strength of spirit and their patriotic virtues.

9

JOSÉ R. MACHADO
AND DUVON C. CORBITT

The Vindication of Carlos J. Finlay as an Element in U.S.–Cuban Relations

Throughout the twentieth century the lack of recognition given to Dr. Carlos J. Finlay by the United States angered sensitive Cubans. For many, the treatment of this renowned scientist became a symbol of the arrogance of the North Americans and a vivid example of how they ignored and distorted Cuban history. For many years these protests in behalf of Finlay were largely ignored, while Walter Reed and William C. Gorgas were extolled as the conquerors of yellow fever in textbooks, en-

Translated from José R. Machado, "Prólogo," to César Rodríguez Expósito, *Finlay: Polémica Permanente* (Havana, Ministerio de Salud Pública, 1961), pp. 5–6, and from Duvon C. Corbitt, "To Carlos J. Finlay on His One Hundred and Twenty-Fifth Anniversary: Let Us Honor This Benefactor of Humanity," *Revista de la Sociedad Cubana de Historia de la Medicina,* I, 4 (Octubre–Diciembre, 1958), 14–16, by permission of the author.

cyclopedias, and the Hall of Fame. The selection which follows by Dr. José R. Machado of the Ministry of Public Health, is a good example of what Cubans have been writing about Finlay for years. It also illustrates how historical errors and intellectual insults can influence relations between nations.

However, some North Americans have worked diligently to correct the record and to give due credit to Finlay for his discovery of the means of transmission of yellow fever. Professor Duvon C. Corbitt has been most active in this campaign. After several years he finally convinced the editors of the *Encyclopedia Americana* to rewrite their article in order to present an accurate account of the battle against yellow fever. In addition, in 1956 he began the process of nominating Dr. Finlay to the Hall of Fame in New York (Finlay had served as a contract surgeon in the U.S. Army during the war with Spain). The Cuban scientist was ruled ineligible, however, and currently Professor Corbitt is working on a proposal to have Congress make Finlay an honorary citizen in order to overcome this obstacle to giving Finlay a place of honor beside Reed and Gorgas. The correction of the historical record in all of its forms so as to remove a standing insult to the Cuban people and to the memory of a great man, is a project which should concern all who are interested in the treatment their country gives to other nations.

[Machado]

The obstinacy of Yankee imperialism is elucidated in the stealing of the legitimate, scientific glory of our Carlos J. Finlay. They extracted from Finlay's discovery a great economic benefit important to them only as a means to exploit unhealthy lands such as Panama, where yellow fever had made it impossible to construct the famous canal. Afterwards they were able to reduce Panamanian sovereignty, just as the Platt Amendment limited and conditioned the liberty and independence of Cuba. And they did this in spite of the fact that the glory of this discovery lies only in its prestige. [It is a prize] which can't be converted to more dividends for dollar imperialism.

Doubtless in their political scorn for the people of the rest of the continent, after they had ignored Finlay, they tried to obscure this discovery. Disregarding his work in order not to have to answer questions about it, they tried to grab the credit and fame for Doctors Walter Reed and William C. Gorgas, whose merit lay in checking and applying Finlay's discovery, after all the forces of three North American commissions had failed to combat the scourge of the black vomit.

. . .

Sixty years have elapsed, yet without doubt—as the historian of the Ministry of Public Health has said—we Cubans are still engaged in a permanent controversy for the vindication of the work and the glory of Finlay. And in the same, fundamental way the North Americans are most interested in ignoring this Cuban scholar, so that Doctors Reed and Gorgas might look all the more illustrious as the conquerors of this terrible scourge, even though a look through their own papers reveals that these men never did believe that the mosquito transmitted yellow fever. Moreover, this historical error is kept alive in the textbooks of North American public and private schools, where Reed is made the hero of a scientific discovery with which he was actually concerned only in a limited fashion. Thus they impress upon youth this lie. Thus they discuss the discovery but have never rectified the error, and so throughout the subsequent decades the error has persisted. The North Americans utilized their economic power and their mediums of publicity to cultivate their own interests, and they did this not only to maintain imperialistic predominance over the peoples of America but, as in this specific case, in order to try to appropriate Cuba's scientific merit.

[Corbitt]

On the night of August 14, 1881, a forty-eight-year-old physician stood on the simple rostrum of the hall of the Cuban Academy of Medico-Physical and Natural Sciences and announced the conclusions he had reached after twenty-three years of study on the cause of yellow fever. He explained the various false leads followed in the years since he began his studies on the disease in 1858, and the reasons why he was now convinced that a transmitting agent was necessary to convey the infection. This agent, according to the conclusions, was the *Culex Fasciata* mosquito (later known also as the *Stegomya Fasciata,* and as the *Aedes Aegypti*).

That August night, which might have been one of triumph for Carlos J. Finlay, for the Academy, and for humanity, was to be one of humiliation, though not of defeat. That simple rostrum is now a national shrine, but there was no indication at the time that such would ever be the case. No one refuted the report presented, no one attempted to prove it correct. For twenty years it was merely disregarded, while thousands suffered needlessly the ravages of yellow fever.

. . .

Dr. Finlay did not stop with his announcements of 1881, but continued to experiment and publish the results in numerous pamphlets, articles, and booklets. These were received with the now customary indifference by his fellows, with the exception of Dr. Claudio Delgado, Dr. Rudolph Matas (then a medical student), and his own professor Dr. Weir Mitchell of Jefferson Medical College. American investigating teams of 1887, 1889, and 1898 spent their efforts on theories advanced by others, while Finlay's conclusions were ignored. Nor did his paper presented to the 1894 Convention of Hygiene and Demography in Budapest find a sympathetic reception, although he specifically outlined the steps necessary to eliminate the danger of infection from yellow fever: to prevent mosquitoes from biting yellow fever patients; to exterminate as many contaminated mosquitoes as possible; and to keep in mind that mosquitoes might live as long as forty days after becoming contaminated.

Twenty years after Dr. Finlay's preliminary announcement in Washington, another physician stood before a learned group in Havana. Dr. Walter Reed was reporting on the classic experiments whereby the American yellow fever commission had demonstrated the truth of Dr. Finlay's announcement of 1881. It was the long delayed hour of triumph for Carlos J. Finlay, for the commission, and for humanity. It was a time of temporary glory for the people of the United States whose representatives in Cuba had vindicated the stand Dr. Finlay had taken for two decades. But, as the application of the discovery spread over the world, the discoverer's name was shifted to the background in the publicity that was given in the United States. Although Dr. Finlay received many honors there, as in other countries, printed accounts of the search for the cause of yellow fever tended to stress the work of the commission, too often without mentioning the discoverer. Treatment of the subject in many standard works of reference did the same, and before long textbooks in science and history followed suit until the one that did justice to Dr. Finlay was the exception. This state of affairs continued for nearly half a century until many abroad doubted the existence of that spirit of fair play of which the people of the United States boast.

Fortunately for the reputation of the American people as lovers of justice, a change has set in. Within the last decade there has been a fine response to the efforts of Finlay admirers to see that his name is honored. Textbooks and reference works are being revised, and there is good reason to believe this injustice will be erased. It is very difficult, however, to counteract an error so widely circulated, but the task must be completed, not only for Dr. Finlay's sake, but also for the sake of the good name of the people of the United States who love justice. The acknowledgement of error will be worth more than many Good Neighbor Policies on paper.

II

❁ ❁ ❁

OBSERVATIONS OF SOCIETY AND CULTURE

10

RICHARD HENRY DANA, JR.

A Boston Yankee's Observations of Religion, Politics, and Society in the Mid-Nineteenth Century

Richard Henry Dana, Jr. gained his first knowledge of Latin America on his voyage from Boston to California (1834–36). His experiences were recorded in *Two Years Before the Mast.* Dana later became a lawyer and an active participant in the Free Soil and Republican parties. In 1859 he went to Cuba and spent almost a month traveling around the island, observing carefully, and taking notes on all he saw and heard. The book which he then wrote is generally accurate and fairly objective; that is, as objective as a nineteenth-century Boston Protestant could be when studying another culture. Dana did not feel that the Cubans were

From Richard Henry Dana, Jr., *To Cuba and Back: A Vacation Voyage* (Boston, Ticknor & Fields, 1859), pp. 225–244, 264, 269.

even close to being ready for self-government. In this he agreed with the strong convictions North Americans would hold until well into the next century.

To an American, from the free States, Cuba presents an object of singular interest. His mind is occupied and almost oppressed by the thought of the strange problems that are in process of solution around him. He is constantly a critic, and a philosophizer, if not a philosopher. A despotic civil government, compulsory religious uniformity, and slavery, are in full possession of the field. He is always seeking information as to causes, processes and effects, and almost as constantly baffled. There are three classes of persons in Cuba, from whom he receives contradictory and irreconcilable statements: the Cubans, the Spaniards, and foreigners of other nations. By Cubans, I mean the Criollos (Creoles), or natives of Cuba. By Spaniards, I mean the Peninsulares, or natives of Old Spain. In the third class are comprised the Americans, English, French, Germans, and all other foreigners, except Spaniards, who are residents on the island, but not natives. This last class is large, possesses a great deal of wealth, and includes a great number of merchants, bankers and other traders.

The Spaniards, or Peninsulares, constitute the army and navy, the officers of the government in all departments, judicial, educational, fiscal and postal, the revenue and the police, the upper clergy, and a large and wealthy class of merchants, bankers, shopkeepers, and mechanics. The higher military and civil officers are from all parts of Spain; but the Catalans furnish the great body of the mechanics and small traders. The Spaniards may be counted on as opponents of the independence of Cuba, and especially of her annexation to the United States. In their political opinions, they vary. Some belong to the liberal, or *Progresista* party, and others are advocates of, or at least apologists for, the present order of things. Their force and influence is increased by the fact that the government encourages its military and civil officers, at the expiration of their terms of service, to remain in the island, still holding some nominal office, or on the pay of a retired list.

The foreign residents, not Spaniards, are chiefly engaged in commerce, banking, or trade, or are in scientific or mechanic employments. These do not intend to become citizens of Cuba. They strike no root into the soil, but feel that they are only sojourners, for purposes of their own. Of all classes of persons, I know of none whose situation is more unfavorable to the growth and development of sentiments of patriotism and philanthropy, and of interest in the future of a race, than foreigners, temporarily resident, for purposes of money-making only, in a country with which they have nothing in common, in the future or the past. This class is often called impartial. I do not agree to that use of the term. They are, indeed, free from the bias of feeling or sentiment; and from the bias generated by the combined action of men thinking and feeling alike, which we call political party. But they are subject to the attractions of interest; and interest will magnetize the mind as effectually as feeling. Planted in a soil where the more tender and delicate fibres can take no hold, they stand by the strong taproot of interest. It is for their immediate advantage to preserve peace and the existing order of things; and even if it may be fairly argued that their ultimate interests would be benefited by a change, yet the process is hazardous, and the result not sure; and, at most, they would do no more than take advantage of the change, if it occurred. I should say, as a general thing, that this class is content with the present order of things. The island is rich, production is large, commerce flourishes, life and property are well protected, and if a man does not concern himself with political or religious questions, he has nothing to fear. Of the Americans in this class, many, doubtless, may be favorably inclined toward annexation, but they are careful talkers, if they are so; and the foreigners, not Americans, are of course earnestly opposed to it, and the pendency of the question tends to draw them towards the present government.

It remains only to speak of the Cubans. They are commonly styled Creoles. But as that word includes natives of all Spanish America, it is not quite definite. Of the Cubans; a few are advocates of the present government,—but very few. The far greater part are disaffected. They desire something approximating to self-government. If that can be had from Spain, they would prefer it. If not, there is nothing for them but independence, or annexation to some other power. Not one of them thinks of independence; and if it be annexation, I believe their present impulse is toward the United States. Yet on this point, even among the most disaffected of the Cubans, there is a difference of opinion. Many of them are sincere emancipationists, and fear that if they come in at the southern end of our Union, that question is closed forever. Others fear that the Anglo-Saxon race would swallow up the power and property of the island, as they have done in California and Texas, and that the Creoles would go to the wall.

. . .

When the liberal constitutions were in force in Spain, in the early part of this century, the benefits of them extended to Cuba. Something like a provincial legislature was established; juntas, or advisory boards and committees, discussed public questions, and made recommendations; a militia was organized; the right to bear arms was recognized; tribunals, with something of the nature of juries, passed upon certain questions; the press was free, and Cuba sent delegates to the Spanish Cortes. This state of things continued, with but few interruptions or variations, to 1825. Then was issued the celebrated

Royal Order of May 29, 1825, under which Cuba has been governed to the present hour. This Royal Order is the only constitution of Cuba. It was probably intended merely as a temporary order to the then Captain-General; but it has been found convenient to adhere to it. It clothes the Captain-General with the fullest powers, the tests and limit of which are as follows:

> . . . fully investing you with the whole extent of power which, by the royal ordinances, is granted to the governors of besieged towns. In consequence thereof, His Majesty most amply and unrestrictedly authorizes your Excellency not only to remove from the island such persons, holding offices from government or not, wherever their occupation, rank, class, or situation in life may be, whose residence there you may believe prejudicial, or whose public or private conduct may appear suspicious to you. . . .

So that, since 1825, Cuba has been not only under martial law, but in a state of siege.

As to the more or less of justice or injustice, of honesty or peculation, of fidelity or corruption, of liberality or severity, with which these powers may have been exercised, a residence of a few days, the reading of a few books, and conversations with a few men, though on both sides, give me no right to pronounce. Of the probabilities, all can judge; especially when we remember that these powers are wielded by natives of one country over natives of another country.

Into the details and anecdotes, and the controversies respecting motives, I do not enter. Certain things we know. Since 1825, there has been no legislative assembly in Cuba, either provincial or municipal. The municipal corporations (ayuntamientos) were formerly hereditary, the dignity was purchasable, and no doubt the bodies were corrupt. But they exercised some control, at least in the levying and expending of taxes; and, being hereditary, were somewhat independent, and might have served, like those of Europe in the middle ages, as nuclei of popular liberties. These have lost the few powers they possessed, and the members are now mere appointees of the Captain-General. Since 1836, Cuba has been deprived of its right to a delegation in the Cortes. Since 1825, vestiges of anything approaching to popular assemblies, juntas, a jury, independent tribunals, a right of voting, or a right to bear arms, have vanished from the island. The press is under censorship; and so are the theatres and opera. When "I Puritani" is played, the singers are required to substitute Lealtà for Libertà, and one singer was fined and imprisoned for recusancy; and Facciolo, the printer of a secretly circulated newspaper, advocating the cause of Cuban independence, was garroted. The power of banishing, without a charge being made, or a trial, or even a record, but on the mere will of the Captain-General, persons whose presence he thinks, or professes to think, prejudicial to the government, whatever their condition, rank, or office, has been frequently exercised, and hangs at all hours over the head of every Cuban. Besides, that terrible power which is restrained only by the analogy of a state of siege, may be at any time called into action. Cubans may be, and I suppose usually are, regularly charged and tried before judges, on political accusations; but this is not their right; and the judges themselves, even of the highest court, the Real Audiencia, may be deposed and banished, at the will of the military chief.

According to the strictness of the written law, no native Cuban can hold any office of honor, trust, or emolument in Cuba. The army and navy are composed of Spaniards, even to the soldiers in the ranks, and to the sailors at the guns. It is said by the supporters of the government that this order is not adhered to; and they point to a captain-general, an intendente, and a chief of the customs, who were Cubans. Still, such is the written law; and if a few Cubans are put into office against the law, those who are so favored are likely to be the most servile of officers, and the situation of the rest is only the more degraded. Notwithstanding the exceptions, it may be said with substantial truth, that an independent Cuban has open to him no career, civil or military. There is a force of volunteers, to which some Cubans are admitted, but they hold their places at the will of the government; and none are allowed to join or remain with them unless they are acceptable to the government.

There are vexatious and mortifying regulations, too numerous and minute to be complied with or even remembered, and which put the people in danger of fines or extortion at every turn. Take, for instance, the regulation that no man shall entertain a stranger over night at his house, without previous notice to the magistrate. As to the absolute prohibition of concealed weapons, and of all weapons but the regulation sword and pistols, it was no doubt introduced and enforced by [Miguel] Tacon as a means of suppressing assassinations, broils and open violence; and it has made life safer in Havana than it is in New York; yet it cannot be denied that it created a serious disability. In fine, what is the Spanish government in Cuba, but an armed monarchy, encamped in the midst of a disarmed and disfranchised people?

The taxes paid by the Cubans on their property, and the duties levied on their commerce, are enormous, making a net income of not less than sixteen million dollars a year. Cuba pays all the expenses of its own government, the salaries of all officers, the entire cost of the army and navy quartered upon it, the maintenance of the Roman Catholic religion, and of all the charitable and benevolent institutions, and sends an annual remittance to Spain.

The number of Spanish men-of-war stationed on the coast varies from twenty-five to thirty. Of the number of soldiers of the regular army in Cuba, it is difficult to form an opinion. The official journal puts them at 30,000. The lowest estimate I heard was 25,000; and the highest was 40,000. Judging from the number of sick I saw at the Hospital Militar, I should not be surprised if the larger estimate was nearer the truth.

Education is substantially in the hands of the government. As an instance of their strictness, no man can take a degree at the University, unless he makes oath that he does not belong to, has never belonged to, and will not belong to, any society not known to and permitted by the government.

But details are of little importance. The actual administration may be a little more or less rigid or lax. In its legal character, the government is an unmixed despotism of one nation over another.

No religion is tolerated but the Roman Catholic. Formerly the church was wealthy, authoritative and independent, and checked the civil and military power by an ecclesiastical power wielded also by the dominant nation. But the property of the church has been sequestrated and confiscated, and the government now owns all the property once ecclesiastical, including the church edifices, and appoints all the clergy, from the bishop to the humblest country curate. All are salaried officers. And so powerless is the church, that, however scandalous may be the life of a parish priest, the bishop cannot remove him. He can only institute proceedings against him before a tribunal over which the government has large control, with a certainty of long delays, and entire uncertainty as to the result. The bishopric of Havana was formerly one of the wealthiest sees in Christendom. Now the salary is hardly sufficient to meet the demands which custom makes in respect of charity, hospitality and style of living. It may be said, I think with truth, that the Roman Catholic Church has now neither civil nor political power in Cuba.

That there was a long period of time during which the morals of the clergy were excessively corrupt, I think there can be no doubt. Make every allowance for theological bias, or for irreligious bias, in the writers and tourists in Cuba, still, the testimony from Roman Catholics themselves is irresistible. The details, it is not worth while to contend about. It is said that a family of children, with a recognized relation to its female head, which the rule of celibacy prevented ever becoming a marriage, was general with the country priesthood. A priest who was faithful to that relation, and kept from cock-fighting and gambling, was esteemed a respectable man by the common people. Cuba became a kind of Botany Bay for the Romish clergy. There they seem to have been concealed from the eye of discipline. With this state of things, there existed, naturally enough, a vast amount of practical infidelity among the people, and especially among the men, who, it is said, scarcely recognized religious obligations at all.

. . .

Of the moral habits of the clergy, as of the people, at the present time, I am entirely unable to judge. I saw very little that indicated the existence of any vices whatever among the people. Five minutes of a street view of London by night, exhibits more vice, to the casual observer, than all Havana for a year. I do not mean to say that the social morals of the Cubans are good, or are bad; I only mean to say that I am not a judge of the question.

The most striking indication of the want of religious control, is the disregard of the Lord's Day. All business seems to go on as usual, unless it be in the public offices. The chain-gang works in the streets, under public officers. House-building and mechanic trades go on uninterrupted; and the shops are more active than ever. The churches, to be sure, are open and well filled in the morning; and I do not refer to amusements and recreations; I speak of public, secular labor. The Church must be held to some responsibility for this. Granted that Sunday is not the Sabbath. Yet, it is a day which, by the rule of the Roman Church, the English Church in England and America, the Greek Church and other Oriental Churches—all claiming to rest the rule on Apostolic authority, as well as by the usage of Protestants on the continent of Europe,—whether Lutherans or Calvinists—is a day of rest from secular labor, and especially from enforced labor. Pressing this upon an intelligent ecclesiastic, his reply to me was that the Church could not enforce the observance; that it must be enforced by the civil authorities; and the civil authorities fall in with the selfishness and gratifications of the ruling classes. And he appealed to the change lately wrought in Paris, in these respects, as evidence of the consistency of his Church. This is an answer, so far as concerns the Church's direct authority; but it is an admission either of feeble moral power, or of neglect of duty in times past. An embarrassment in the way of more strictness as to secular labor, arises from the fact that slaves are entitled to their time on Sundays, beyond the necessary labor of providing for the day; and this time they may use in working out their freedom.

Another of the difficulties the church has to contend with, arises out of negro slavery. The Church recognizes the unity of all races, and allows marriage between them. The civil law of Cuba, under the interpretations in force here, prohibits marriage between whites and persons who have any tinge of the black blood. In consequence of this rule, concubinage prevails, to a great extent, between whites and mulattoes or quadroons, often with recognition of the children. If either party to this arrangement comes under the influence of the Church's discipline, the relation must terminate. The Church would allow and advise marriage; but the law prohibits it—and if there should be a separation, there may be no provisions for the children. This state of things creates no small obstacle to the influence of the Church over the domestic relations.

. . .

As to education, I have no doubt that a good education in medicine, and a respectable course of instruction in the Roman and Spanish law, and in the natural sciences, can be obtained at the University of Havana; and that a fair collegiate education, after the manner of the Latin races, can be obtained at the Jesuit College, the Seminario, and other institutions at Havana, and in the other large cities; and the Sisters of the Sacred Heart have a flourishing school for girls at Havana. But the general elementary education of the people is in a very low state. The scattered life of planters is unfavorable to public day-schools, nay, almost inconsistent with their existence. The richer inhabitants send their children abroad, or to Havana: but the middle and lower classes of whites cannot do this. The tables show that of the free white children, not more than one in sixty-three attend any school, while in the British West India islands, the proportion is from one in ten to one in twenty. As to the state of education, culture and literary habits among the upper classes, my limited experience gives me no opportunity to judge. The concurrent testimony of tourists and other writers on Cuba is, that the habits of the Cuban women of the upper and middle classes are unintellectual.

. . .

The natural process for Cuba is an amelioration of her institutions under Spanish auspices. If this is not to be had, or if the connection with Spain is dissolved in any way, she will probably be substantially under the protection of some other power, or a part of another empire. Whatever nation may enter upon such an undertaking as this, should take a bond of fate. Beside her internal danger and difficulties, Cuba is implicated externally with every cause of jealousy and conflict. She has been called the key to the Gulf of Mexico. But the Gulf of Mexico cannot be locked. Whoever takes her is more likely to find in her a key to Pandora's box.

11

ROLAND T. ELY

The "Golden Age" of the Hacendado: Society and Culture in the Late Colonial Period

During the mid-nineteenth century creole society in Cuba reached its apex. The sugar economy was flourishing, the Negro population was increasing rapidly, and the social structure of the island reflected these developments. Scholars differ in their interpretation of the effect of these changes on modern Cuba (see the selections by Fernando Ortiz [Document 20] and Sidney Mintz [Document 21]). Ramiro Guerra believed that the major problems of concentration of land ownership developed later, and that the Cuba of this period was characterized by the "largest, hardiest, most prosperous, and

From Roland T. Ely, *Cuando Reinaba su Majestad el Azucar* (Buenos Aires, Editorial Sudamericana, 1963), pp. 696–697, 717, 724–726, 742–745, 779–783, 786–789. Reprinted by permission of the author.

most enterprising class of rural proprietors in its history."[1] Yet this was also a period in which these Cubans were isolated from the responsibilities of political leadership.

Professor Ely's analysis of the society of the upper-class landowners indicates that some Cuban problems did originate in this era. The opulence and extravagance of these "lords of the manor" helped to mold an upper-class cultural psychology which reinforced (or even revived in some cases) the aristocratic elements in the Hispanic tradition. Thus the Cuban upper class was poorly prepared for the problems of an industrial and technological age, and this has posed one of the dilemmas of the twentieth century.

Professor Roland T. Ely is on the faculty of the economics department at Rutgers University. He has travelled extensively in Latin America, and has been decorated by several governments for his services to the cause of inter-American understanding.

As a class . . . the *hacendados* of Cuba were intelligent, well-travelled and often highly refined; . . . their generous hospitality could border upon the prodigal. . . . Meanwhile, conspicuous among their other distinguishing traits was an inordinate love of pure ostentation. Devotion to display for its own sake swept many a fine old creole family into dangerous extravagances; often to financial ruin. Preoccupation with the materialistic frequently prevented members of the proprietary class from taking advantage of the almost unlimited cultural opportunities which their monetary resources made possible. Not that their North American neighbors happened to be any less ostentatious, especially during the so-called

[1] Ramiro Guerra y Sánchez, *Sugar and Society*, p. 49.

ROCHESTER INSTITUTE OF TECHNOLOGY LIBRARY

"Gilded Age," but foreign visitors appear to have been particularly impressed by the extent to which this tendency asserted itself in Queen Isabel II's Cuba.

Sensible of "the Cuban population's display and ostentation," Morelet reached an obvious conclusion in 1846: ". . . that in a country where the aspirations of society are primarily directed toward the cult of wealth, letters and the sciences enjoy little favor." For all his alacrity to accept "American hospitality" in Cuba, Ramón de la Sagra had some harsh things to say, particularly about the people of Cienfuegos:

> Life, for the majority of its inhabitants, is spent between the arrival of *hogsheads of sugar* and the shipment of *hogsheads of sugar;* for which reason, my friend [there] used to say that . . . the *God Hogshead* was the divinity worshipped in Cienfuegos.

One evening a distinguished Cuban lady complained to him:

> But here, materialism is gross, purely practical, convenient, egotistical . . . it absorbs, dominates and smothers the intellectual, without leaving a single breath for the great and the sublime.

• • •

Given the Cuban planters' penchant for ostentation, it was to be expected that many of them should have sought patents of nobility and other honors from the Spanish Crown. Possessed of princely estates in the country and extravagant establishments in town and abroad, nothing seemed more natural than to formalize their high station in colonial society with a title of *conde* or *marqués*. Unlike some countries in Europe, where the nobility still retained a measure of political influence, it was little more than an honorary order in Cuba. As García de Arboleya indicated a century ago,

> Here [in Cuba] the nobility does not constitute an element of power; but it is represented in the Court

> by some of its members elevated to the dignity of Senators of the Kingdom. It can be considered as divided into two classes: the dignities and the titles of Castile. . . .

. . .

Julio, Marqués de Apezteguia, was but one of many "sugar noblemen" who illustrated the ephemeral nature of this species. . . . By the eighties he was sitting in the Spanish Cortes as a Conservative Deputy from Santa Clara [now Las Villas] Province. During the same decade, he also gained control of "Constancia" and transformed the old family *ingenio* into a modern *central;* so successfully, in fact, that it was described as "the largest in the world" in 1889. Indeed, so famous had this estate become, that John Prince's *Cuba Illustrated* made a special point of advising readers: "American tourists should not fail to visit this immense plantation."

Perhaps it was only fitting that American tourists take a look around "Constancia." By the early 'nineties, control of this property had largely slipped into the hands of their own countrymen. Though Julio had progressed from Deputy to Senator in the Cortes and become leader of the Conservative Party in Cuba—not to mention his title of Marqués de Apezteguia in 1891—these were expensive honors, even for the proprietor of Central "Constancia." . . .

In 1894, for instance, he had already lost direct control of his magnificent central. Its management had been taken over by the Constancia Sugar Co., of 41 Wall Street, which held a large mortgage on the estate. Five of the company's seven directors were Americans; the next year six. So it went, until "Constancia" soon belonged entirely to the New York syndicate. Once again the old Spanish proverb (*padre bodeguero, hijo caballero, nieto pordiosero*) was fulfilled, and another Cuban fortune vanished within three generations. Apart from a few of the older inhabitants around Cienfuegos, practically no one in Cuba today can recall that the Apezteguia family ever existed. . . .

. . .

Plainly, it lies beyond the scope of this work to conduct a sociological investigation of the proprietary class in Cuba . . . At the same time, however, certain facets of the creole character attracted so much attention among foreign visitors during the last century that no survey of criollo society in the Cuban sugar industry's Golden Age can completely ignore them.

One might begin almost anywhere. Mercedes de Santa Cruz would be as good a place as any. Born and raised in one of the island's most prominent creole families, she later married a French general and spent much of her adult life abroad. When she visited Cuba as the Countess of Merlin some years afterward, it was possible for her to view the island with a degree of objectivity which would have been very difficult for the average Cuban aristocrat. Early in the forties, for example, she ventured to observe that:

> One of the peculiar characteristics of the present race of Spaniards in Havana, European plants transplanted to the island, is the contrast which exists between the languidness of their small and delicate bodies, incapable of suffering the least fatigue, and the ardor of their blood . . .

From such evidence—and there is no dearth of contemporary accounts—one would logically conclude that the Caucasian race underwent some sort of mutation after two or three generations in Cuba. For the male members of the island's slave-supported aristocracy, there appears to have been some justification for this belief. "Degeneracy and disaffection invariably set in at the second or third generation; and nothing is more common," declared Gallenga (an Italian), "than to see the son of the stoutest merchant or planter of Spanish origin, especially if born of a Cuban mother, contract the habits and feelings of the natives."

. . .

These remarks had the familiar ring of post-mortems on the planter class elsewhere, as in Jamaica. Sagra (a peninsular Spaniard) reminded his friends on the Pearl of the Antilles that: "There are conditions in modern civilization, which impose imperative obligations upon the wealthy classes who, believing they have an innate right to be conspicuous only by the ostentation of their riches, do nothing for the general culture. . . ."

Perhaps it was the soft climate, perhaps the enervating influences inherent in a society supported by several hundred thousand Negro slaves. "We will endeavor to see him as he is," said James Steele, United States Consul for six years in Cuba, "the Creole, the tropical white man, possibly entitled to be regarded as the founder of a race." As Steele saw the upper-class Cuban criollo:

> This man is the born dandy . . . Born in a slave country, the presumptive, possible or actual heir to a share in some sugar plantation, or, if not, living by his wits or upon his relations, the young Cuban imagines that his destiny is to ornament the tropics; to be a thing of beauty, and kill time while he is thus elegantly occupied.

This predilection "to ornament the tropics" seems to have caused considerable friction in Cuba between criollo and peninsular. Edwin F. Atkins, for example, observed much bad feeling ". . . in the Cienfuegos business houses [where] most of the clerks were Spaniards, hard-working and frugal, who despised the luxurious, indolent Cubans." Of course, the poverty-ridden Spanish immigrant had no choice but to work so that a certain amount of his hatred obviously stemmed from sheer envy of the Cuban planter's material wealth. Yet even where such motives did not exist, as with foreign tourists who had no desire to become rich *hacendados* themselves, there was a tendency to censure the indolence which characterized a large portion of the proprietary class.

. . .

Doubtless many Cubans regretted that their calendar did not schedule Carnival (or some other officially sanctioned saturnalia) every week of the year. Wealthy criollos were able to avoid such frustrations, of course. If so inclined, they could make every night a Saturday in Havana, and Saturday a New Year's Eve. Members of the proprietary class who drifted into the capital's fast set had ample scope there for various forms of self-indulgence.

Setting out on an evening stroll, for instance, one could cross the Plaza de Isabella and find several fashionable cafés near the Tacon Theatre. These were the spots, in the words of a foreign observer, ". . . where 'life' commences at nine o'clock in the evening and rages fast and furious until the small hours of the morning." He also noted that it was not always easy to find a seat in such places, because: "In these resorts, which are one blaze of light, every gas-burner reflected by dozens of mirrors, the marble tables are all occupied by vivacious patrons."

To name one, there was the Dominica, "a kind of exchange where strangers meet, eat, drink, and smoke." Native sons of the island were accustomed to the choking fumes sent forth by scores of "Long Toms" and the daintier *cigarillos*. Foreigners were not. Surveying this café in 1855, a well-travelled Carolinian complained that, "The dense smoke arising from the rich Habana [leaf] makes my head swim." Closer inspection revealed that many of the ladies present were making generous personal contributions to the rank clouds of tobacco smoke which billowed into every nook and cranny of the large, pulsating establishment. At first, he was fascinated by "the smoke curling in the air from their delicate coquettish lips." But he soon learned that one came to take these things for granted in Cuba, as ". . . such is the life in this Spanish town—men and women are free and easy in their manner, especially the married ladies."

. . .

. . . Returning to Philadelphia after several years of residence on the Great Antille during the late sixties, a veteran of the recent war between the states felt obliged to caution his fellow countrymen about a number of surprises they would encounter in Cuba. Among them he mentioned that:

> The sensitive stranger will be frequently shocked, as, passing through some even of the principal streets, after dark, he has his attention called by some dark-eyed syren—frequently very handsome, too—who winningly invites him to enter her domicile, and pay his respects to some of the many richly dressed women he finds seated in the *sala* [parlor], and who can be easily and sufficiently seen through the bars of the open window in passing.

By this time, however, Havana's sultry sirens of the tropic night were confronted with some serious competition for the attentions of free-spending criollos. Contemporary accounts suggest that more and more of their erring sisters from the North were infiltrating the Pearl of the Antilles each year that went by. . . .

. . .

. . . By then [1865] the influx of American courtesans was reaching formidable proportions. Steamships had shrunk the voyage between New York and Havana to five days in the late sixties. The island of Cuba had never been more prosperous. If sporting members of the planter class tossed away dozens of doubloons on the outcome of one cockfight, a contest that might be settled against them in less than half an hour; if wealthy hacendados risked a whole year's crop upon the turn of a single card, it followed that some of them should be willing to part with a little gold to enjoy a far more ancient diversion. The stakes were high; the distance short.

But bold as their attack upon the lords of King Sugar's Caribbean domain may have been, quite a few *americanas* fell short of the goal. "It is sad to relate that many of our own countrywomen, lured out here in hopes of gaining large sums from the wealthy Spaniards, come only to find themselves a more despised and unfortunate class than they were in their own country . . . ," said Samuel Hazard . . .

"Variety's the very spice of life," commented William Cowper in the preceding century. From the popularity which northern women appear to have enjoyed among Cuban criollos one concludes that those who could afford imported American "spice" were inclined to agree with the celebrated British bard. The Cuban male can still fully appreciate a fine pair of sparkling blue eyes, crowned with luxuriant golden tresses, if for no other reason than the contrast which they offer to the profusion of dark, raven-haired beauty that surrounds him at home. Thus for over a century predatory americanas have been trying to reap "a rich harvest"—to borrow one of "Deputy's" expressions—from the cane fields of Cuba.

Scarcely a year after "Deputy" wrote of Josephine Stuart's suicide in "the notorious Cerro restaurant," the Golden Age of the Cuban sugar planter came to an end.[2] On 10 October 1868, Carlos Manuel de Céspedes issued a call to arms against Spanish rule and thus began the bloody but indecisive Ten Years War. Since then some thirteen hundred ingenios have given way to less than two hundred modern sugar factories with the evolution of the central system. Chauffeur-driven, air-conditioned Cadillacs have replaced the lumbering *volantes* and their

---

[2] Josephine Stuart was a native of Kentucky who became one of Havana's leading prostitutes. She shot herself in a fit of despondency over a departed lover. [ed.]

liveried outriders. New York is but five hours away from Havana by pressurized, four-engined giants of the sky; Miami a mere forty-five minutes.

Yet with all these changes, the behavior of certain elements within the group which profited most from Cuba's rich agricultural resources remained much the same until Fidel Castro appeared upon the Cuban scene. Meanwhile, many of those who came down from the North to join various members of the upper class at play might have been described as follows: "American shoddyism . . . mustering very strong here this winter season, and coming in for more than its share of the gaudy pageantry." Upwards of a century has elapsed since Antonio Gallenga wrote these words. But anyone who has had occasion to pass some time in Havana or to visit Varadero's incomparable beach near Cárdenas, might reluctantly conclude that Gallenga's comment held equally true until January 1959.

12

RICHARD PATTEE

The Role of the Roman Catholic Church

In spite of the fact that most Cubans are nominally associated with the Roman Catholic Church, this institution has not been a major force in Cuba in modern times. The Church was severely weakened during the latter part of the colonial period, and even lost much of the property which had been acquired earlier. This helps to explain the comparative lack of anti-clericalism in Cuba. During the twentieth century the Church has tried to establish itself as a positive social force, but these efforts have been hampered by a chronic shortage of priests—especially in rural areas—and by the fact that many priests were Spaniards with a pro-Franco orientation.

With perceptive insight Professor Richard Pattee argued in 1946 that the major problem facing the Church was that of maladjustments in the social and

From Richard Pattee and the Inter-American Committee, *Catholic Life in the West Indies* (Washington, D.C.: 1946), pp. 18–21, 27–28, 30–31. Reprinted by permission of the Catholic Association for International Peace.

economic order. Whether or not the Church in Cuba could have been a more effective agent for reform is still an open question, but a recent work on the subject concluded: "The Church did not plan for change, but for stability; when revolution finally came, it was the last thing the hierarchy was prepared for."[1]

Professor Pattee served as one of the chairmen of the Inter-American Committee of the Catholic Association for International Peace. He has written several books dealing with Latin America and Portugal, and is currently teaching in Laval University in Quebec, Canada.

. . . The independence of Cuba was a violent and disruptive influence on the relations of the Church and the state. Under Spanish rule the relations of the two entities had been very close. Cuba exemplified the usual arrangement that prevailed between the Spanish state and the Catholic Church. The most serious angle of the case in Cuba was not, however, the purely technical one of the juridical relation, but the much more important one of the position of the Church and its clergy toward independence and the fact that in the popular mind, the Church had been closely identified with the old regime. The Cuban hierarchy prior to independence was entirely Spanish. The number of Cuban priests and religious was small in comparison with the Spanish. As a colony it was natural that the overwhelming majority of the clergy should be from Spain. It was equally reasonable, although certainly not entirely fortunate, that this clergy and hierarchy should feel the tug of the mother country when it came to a showdown between Cuban independence or

[1] Leslie Dewart, *Christianity and Revolution: The Lesson of Cuba* (New York, 1963), p. 101.

continued attachment to Spain. Many of the clergy became identified with the status quo, although the exceptions were numerous. In no sense could the first Cuban republic of Carlos Manuel de Céspedes or the later successful movement be considered as anti-clerical or much less anti-Catholic. In Cuba as elsewhere in Hispanic America the nineteenth century was strongly tinged in its thinking with liberalism and secularism. Much of the absence of anti-Catholic feeling may justly be attributed more to the prevalence of the secularist mentality than to any deliberate respect for the Church. The story of the infiltration and flowering of secularism in the Cuba of the last century would be a long story and entirely beyond the scope of this brochure.

One of the most active influences in the long incubation of Cuban independence was the Masonic lodges. The *logias* very frequently supplied the underground, the "resistance," to use the modern phrase, and the conspiratorial climate so necessary for the carrying out of the program of opposition to the established government. The consequence was that Masonry took for itself much of the credit for the severance of the ties with Spain and by the same logic attributed to the Church a systematic antagonism to that independence. This particular conception of the history of Cuba has prevailed down to the present time in some circles. Little has been done until very recently by Catholics to dispel this impression and clarify the true role of the Church in the emancipation and later independent existence of the country. The real problem of Cuban Catholicism becomes evident in this brief exposition of some of the antecedents. With the break-up of the old order, the Church was seriously threatened in its mission. Seminaries, schools and colleges were interrupted or in some instances destroyed. Chapels and churches fell into disuse and in the countryside ravaged by the constant movements of the insurgents, normal religious life was all but suspended. The Church was forced to begin in 1900 the slow process of re-establishing its influence, winning back areas temporarily lost and above all of demonstrating that it belonged to *independent* Cuba in the same manner as it had belonged to *colonial* Cuba.

. . .

The change of regime and the transitory American military government under General Leonard Wood posed some serious problems for the Church. The question of civil marriage, the secularization of the cemeteries, the future of Church property and the like were all problems that required more or less immediate attention. It was part of the readjustment that set in with the disappearance of the former Spanish government with which, for four centuries, these relations had become completely defined. The Spanish government had had, nevertheless, its difficulties in the business of properties. The Concordat of 1861 had settled the matter to some degree. This instrument provided among other things that the Spanish government would pay the Church an annual rent for the properties that the state had taken for secular use. General Wood arrived at what was considered broadly to be a reasonably satisfactory settlement, bearing in mind the perfectly legitimate interests of the Church.

It is sometimes said that Cuba has never known the religious problem. This generally means that Cuba has never known the violent anti-clerical outbursts or actual civil war over religious questions that have devastated some of the other republics. In the convention of 1900 which formulated the new Cuban constitution, it was evident, however, that the religious issue was very much in the fore. There was definite antagonism to the Church. There were evidences of an incipient anti-clericalism. The decision on the religious question revealed that Cuba was to be henceforth a nation in which state and Church were absolutely separated. The state assumes no obligations for the support of the Church, and contributes nothing to the maintenance of its institutions or establishments. For all practical purposes the relations of the Cuban government to the Catholic Church are the same as that of the government of the United States to the Church. There is the difference, nevertheless, that the great majority of the Cuban people are Catholics; they know no other religion and as a result, whenever there is the admission of any religious influence whatever in public acts or in government affairs it is, of course, a Catholic one. When President Ramón Grau San Martín was inaugurated recently, he followed the custom of having present the Archbishop of La Habana, the highest dignitary of the Church in the republic. There was criticism from some sources that this revealed favoritism toward the Church and that the various evangelical sects in the country should also have been given an invitation. It may be said that the Cuban government has never been animated by any prejudice against the Church. Many of the presidents have been quite favorable to it. Anticlericalism has existed only in a limited sense which must be described briefly in order to avoid confusion with similar manifestations in such republics as Colombia, Ecuador or Mexico. In Cuba, there has been some tendency to level criticism against members of the clergy who are Spanish. The question has become more an animosity against a nationality than against a religion. The number of the clergy who are Spanish is still very large especially in the religious communities. Many of the leading colleges and schools are in their hands. Two members of the Cuban hierarchy are Spaniards. This question has been complicated by the events since 1936: the Spanish Civil War, the activities of the Falange, the suspicion that many of the Spaniards sympathized too openly with the Franco regime.

Under Cuban law there is no limitation on the activities of other religions. Protestant denominations have been free to establish themselves in the republic and have taken advantage of the liberality of the legislation. Today evangelical sects flourish all over the country. Their colleges are in some cases particularly outstanding as in Cárdenas and in Habana itself. The Catholic Church has been given no aid, no support and no official encouragement. It has had to make its own way as best it could. The important thing to remember is that the Church has had to fight its way back to a position of prestige after a very severe body blow in 1900. It began under serious handicaps and it is thus not surprising that it has taken many years before Catholic Action and especially Catholic social thinking could take root and develop. Only since 1930 has there been anything in this line of real significance.

. . .

Late in 1942, *Democracia Social Cristiana* issued a formal program, stating its aims and aspirations. The Archbishop of Habana, Monsignor Manuel Arteaga y Betancourt, gave it his blessing and entire support. The most considerable Catholic social movement in Cuba was launched and one of the most interesting experiments in Latin America was getting under way. The leading Habana daily, *Diario de la Marina,* considered it as the most adequate reply to the extremisms which were becoming more and more popular in Cuba. The Communist daily *Hoy* struck the sour note with the usual condemnation of the movement as fascist, falangist, fifth-columnist and totalitarian in general.

The program of the movement may be summarized as follows, translating from the official statement of the program. It is not a political party nor does it have any interest whatever in elections or in party politics. It is purely an ideological movement on behalf of social and economic principles. It condemns economic individualism which it interprets as the supremacy of capital over labor and it also condemns collectivism as the domination of labor over capital. *Democracia Social Cristiana* aspires to bring about a socio-economic order in which the principles of Christian teachings, of charity and justice may be the determining factors. . . .

. . .

. . . The Communist question is not an academic one in Cuba. One of the forms it has taken has been an assault on private education. Cuban public opinion has been considerably agitated by the debate over the proposal popularly known as the Marinello Law, introduced by Senator Juan Marinello, President of the Popular Socialist party, the present name of the Communist party. This party pretends to interpret the articles of the Constitution on education in such a manner as to place all education under the supervision and control of the state—not merely in terms of inspection but also for the determination of content, which would be literally that the private institutions in which religion is taught would suffer severely. Other attempts in terms of the nationality of the teaching staffs have been raised in the attempt to exclude non-Cubans from teaching, a fact which would play havoc with most of the Catholic schools where many of the staff are either foreign born or naturalized Cubans.

It is a very positive reality. The Catholic Church is fully aware of this and has been developing the means of combatting the infiltration of Communism. It must always be borne in mind that Communism in Cuba thrives because of the extraordinary maladjustments in the economic and social order; the absence of sufficient forces to express concern for the plight of the lowly and the humble; the fact that thousands of *guajiros* or peasants, live a hand to mouth existence in the rural areas with little hope of betterment for themselves and their families. In the urban centers, the problem of the proletariat has become acute. Workers on the docks, in the industries and in the sugar mills are bound to feel the impact of Communism if no other agency or doctrine is presented to them. For this reason, the importance of the work of the Catholic organizations mentioned above is singularly opportune. They need above all encouragement from abroad, help and aid in every form. They are laboring as is the case in most of the Latin American countries on a very narrow margin. . . .

13

WILLIAM R. BASCOM

The African Heritage and Its Religious Manifestations

The problem of cultural diversity in modern Cuba has been accentuated by the strong African heritage retained by a sizable minority of the population. This has been somewhat obscured by the apparent religious homogeneity of the populace. Professor William R. Bascom has probed behind the facade and uncovered a basic divergence of belief which has complicated the process of building a unified Cuban society.

Professor Bascom is a social anthropologist who has served on the faculty of Northwestern University for several years. He has done field work in Africa and the Caribbean.

From William R. Bascom, "The Focus of Cuban Santeria," *Southwestern Journal of Anthropology,* VI, 1 (Spring, 1950), 64–68. Reprinted by permission of the *Southwestern Journal of Anthropology* and of the author.

The worship of African deities, as it is practised in Cuba today, is known as *santeria.* The deities and the men and women who work with them are known by the Spanish words *santos, santeros,* and *santeras,* or by the Yoruba words *orisha, babalorisha,* and *iyalorisha.* Santeria is a vital, growing institution, practised throughout the entire length of the island, in both rural and urban areas; in the latter, in fact, it is probably the strongest. In recent years it seems to have been expanding, recruiting additional members from the Negro, the mixed, and even the white population.

The African elements of santeria are predominantly Yoruba, or Lucumi, as the Yoruba of Nigeria are called in Cuba. In the town of Jovellanos, Matanzas province, where most of the material on which this paper is based was gathered, the importance of Yoruba religion in santeria is clearly apparent. The Yoruba influence is also recognizable throughout Cuba, despite regional variations, in the names of the Yoruba deities, in similarities to Yoruba ritual, in the Yoruba cities named by Cuban Negroes as homes of their ancestors, and in individuals who can still speak the Yoruba language. On a quick trip in the summer of 1948, more than eighty years after slavery, it was possible to find Cuban Negroes in towns from one end of the island to the other, and in Havana itself, with whom I could talk in Yoruba.

Certain features of santeria have become well known through the work of Herskovits and other scholars in the field of New World Negro studies. In Cuba they have been discussed in the valuable contributions of Ortiz and of Lachatanere, Castellanos, and Martín. These features include the syncretism of African deities with Catholic saints, commonly represented by chromolithographs; the African pattern of possession which has attracted interest as a psychological phenomenon; and the retention of animal sacrifices and African drumming, singing, and dancing in the New World Negro rituals. All of these are important elements in Cuban santeria, but in the mind of the cult members in Jovellanos, those which are the foundations of their form of worship are the stones, the blood, and the herbs.

. . .

The fundamental importance of the stones in Cuban santeria was stressed consistently by informants. While chromolithographs and plaster images of the Catholic saints are prominently displayed in the shrines and houses of the santeros, they are regarded only as empty ornaments or decorations, which may be dispensed with. The real power of the santos resides in the stones, hidden behind a curtain in the lower part of the altar, without which no santeria shrine could exist. The stones of the saints are believed to have life. Some stones can walk and grow, and some can even have children. Informants told of their own experiences with stones which they had thrown into the streets or otherwise disposed of, only to have them reappear in the house. The most powerful stones are said to have been brought from Africa by the slaves, who concealed them in their stomachs by swallowing them.

The power of the stones is conceived as an invisible fluid, whose force at times can be felt. This is the power which protects the santero and the members of his cult house, and through which the "guardian angel" or saint manifests its blessings. This miraculous power is given to the stones by treating them with the two other essentials of santeria, herbs and blood. This treatment is known as "baptism" (*bautismo*). Stones which have not been prepared in this way, as well as any item of cult paraphernalia which has not been "baptized," are called "Jewish" (*judia*); they are said to be distasteful to the saints, as well as completely powerless.

When he acquires his stones, each santero takes an oath to protect them constantly and to feed them at least annually. When the saints are fed, the warm blood of the sacrificial animals is allowed to flow onto the stones. The blood must be *caliente* or warm, so that the invisible fluid of the stones may be increased. Following the blood sacrifices there is drumming, singing, and dancing, usually for three successive nights, during which the possessions take place. A large number of possessions is desirable because it is a sign that the saints are well fed and satisfied, and also because the fluid and power of the stones are increased by the presence of saints in possession. The major cult rituals of santeria center about the annual feeding of the saints through the stones.

. . .

Each saint has its own particular herbs, its own type of stone, and special animals which are its favorite food. The function of the herbs is to cleanse and refresh and to prepare individuals or objects for contact with the saints. The blood is the food of the saints. The stones are the objects through which the saints are fed, and in which their power resides. One might perhaps find parallels to these three elements in the consecrated stone (*el ara*) in the Catholic altar, in the blood of Christ as symbolized in the Eucharist, and in the burned palm leaves used on Ash Wednesday. The differences, however, are so marked that one may safely say that the blood, the stones, and the herbs as they are employed in santeria are foreign to Catholicism.

. . .

We may then, take the use of stones, blood, and herbs in santeria as African in origin and turn to the second and more important problem. Is the emphasis on these three elements as the focus of Cuban santeria also derived from Africa? Here we can speak with less assurance in terms of our present knowledge of West Africa. On the basis of my own field work among the Yoruba, stones (or *iponri*), blood, and herbs do not seem to assume the importance that they hold in the minds of Jovellanos worshippers. The mythology or theology of the gods, the prayers and the verbal formulæ, and the rituals themselves seem of equal, if not greater importance. . . .

. . .

Another possibility, however, presents itself: that in contact with Catholicism, the distinctive features of African religion, which set santeria apart from the rituals of the Church, have been given additional emphasis and have come to be regarded as the core of the religion. In other words, the focal elements of Cuban santeria may not represent a carry-over of the focus of West African religion, but a shift in emphasis which has occurred as a result of culture contact. In this instance, acculturation would have resulted, not in a coalescence of beliefs, such as is represented by the syncretism of African deities and Catholic saints, the use of plaster images, chromolithographs, candles, and holy water, or the recitation of the Lord's Prayer and Hail Mary in santeria rituals, but a shift in the opposite direction. The present evidence is largely negative, but this interpretation is at least plausible.

If it is correct, an interesting psychological point is raised, since the members of santeria cults regard themselves as Catholics. All informants, without exception, stated unqualifiedly that they were Catholics, yet they stressed the importance of those very elements of their faith and ritual which set it apart from that of the Catholic Church. This would seem to be another illustration of Herskovits' concept of ambivalence in New World Negro cultures. While Catholicism is outwardly embraced, it is inwardly rejected; and the stones, the blood, and the herbs have become, perhaps unconsciously, a rallying point for the defense of the African religious tradition.

14

FOREIGN POLICY ASSOCIATION

Ethnic Composition of the Island's Population and Problems of Cultural Conflict

In 1934 the Foreign Policy Association sent a group of scholars to Cuba to conduct a study in depth of the problems of the island. The published findings of this group (edited by Raymond L. Buell) constituted the most extensive survey of socio-economic conditions in Cuba ever made. This group also recommended various changes, such as land reform, economic diversification, and the evacuation of the Guantánamo naval base by the U.S. Fifteen years later, however, the mission of the International Bank for Reconstruction and Development found that numerous conditions men-

From Raymond L. Buell, *et al.*, *Problems of the New Cuba* (New York, Foreign Policy Association, 1935), excerpts from pp. 28–37. Reprinted by permission of the Foreign Policy Association.

tioned in the earlier report remained virtually unchanged.

Racial Elements

When discovered by Columbus, Cuba was inhabited by Indian peoples, chief of which were the Ciboneyes and Tainan Arawaks. These Indians offered little resistance to the Spanish Conquistador. Reduced to slavery, the Cuban Indian population was exterminated by the middle of the sixteenth century. Unlike other Latin-American countries, Cuba does not have a *mestizo* population based on a mixture of Spanish and Indian blood, nor does it have a large unassimilated Indian population, like Guatemala and Mexico. While this fact has deprived Cuba of the native arts which characterize the life of other Latin-American nations, it may have freed the island from the acute social problems found in countries which have attempted to blend Indian and Spanish culture.

History, however, has bequeathed to Cuba an important Negro problem. Following the destruction of the Indian population, the government of Spain authorized a limited importation of Negro slaves from Africa into Cuba in 1517. As a result of a slave monopoly, represented by successive concessions or *asientos,* only about sixty thousand slaves were imported into Cuba before 1763.

Following the British occupation of Havana, restrictions on this commerce were gradually removed in response to the demand for labor caused by improved economic conditions. It is estimated that altogether, until the abolition of the slave trade, more than a million Africans were carried to Cuba. It was this Negro population which provided most of the labor in the development of the sugar industry.

Beginning with 1814 England induced Spain to sign a series of treaties promising to abolish the slave traffic in return for a payment by England which, in an agreement of 1817, was fixed at £400,000. Instead of enforcing these agreements, Spanish officials in Cuba speculated in contraband slave traffic. Following a slave insurrection, the Spanish government enacted a law in 1845 suppressing the slave trade, but this law only partially stopped the illicit traffic.

It was the Cuban revolutionists in the Ten Years' War who took the initiative in abolishing slavery. In 1869 the Cuban revolutionary assembly at Guáimaro provided for the abolition of such slavery on condition that compensation be granted to the owner. Following the restoration of peace, Spain likewise abolished slavery in a law of February 3, 1880. The law declared that for a period of ten years the slaves should continue under a state of serfdom or *patronato*. The patrons had the right to use the labor of the Negro during this period, but in return were obliged to feed, clothe and compensate the Negroes for their labor, and educate their children. In 1886 the patronato system was abolished, and thereafter the Negro slaves became legally free.

As a result of the importation of Negro slaves and, to a certain extent, the natural increase, the colored population of Cuba in 1817 and 1841 exceeded in number the white population. Confronted with the example of the slave insurrection in Haiti, many white Cubans as well as North Americans opposed the idea of a Cuban republic, fearing that it would be dominated by blacks.

Statistics, however, show that the proportion of colored to white population has steadily declined to the point where today it constitutes 27 percent of the total. Assimilation between Negroes and whites has proceeded so rapidly that this figure cannot be regarded as wholly accurate. The number of mulattoes has steadily increased, while that of pure Negroes has steadily declined. Many mulattoes now pass as white Cubans, and it is consequently difficult for the census to make accurate distinctions. Some Cuban observers believe that not more than half of the total population is pure white.

The presence of a large body of Negroes whose roots go back to Africa inevitably has left a mark on the life of Cuba. These Negroes have continued to perform the manual labor to which they had become accustomed under slavery. In the towns they are found in domestic service, in the ports many of them work as stevedores, in the sugar country Negroes cut a large part of the sugar cane. The colored element in the population has introduced a psychology and mode of life common to Negroes in other parts of the world. Still retaining many of the customs of an African background, which in a new environment have lost their meaning, a considerable part of the Negroes have not been completely assimilated into Cuban culture. As a result, a psychological conflict has come into existence, aggravated by the misery in which many Negroes live. In the days of slavery many Negroes in Cuba practiced fetishism, and today numerous *ñáñigo* secret societies and other animistic cults may be found.

Occupying the bottom of the social scale, and with little opportunity for social or economic advancement, the Negroes provide numerous recruits for the Cuban underworld. According to the 1932 statistics, a racial group containing 27 percent of the population was responsible for about 50 percent of the serious crime. Negroes have been the object of particular solicitude on the part of the Communists, and some of them took the lead in the radical strikes which swept Cuba in 1933–1934. Although among all the lower classes of Cuba "free unions" or common-law marriages are not unusual, the percentage of Negroes who live under extra-legal matrimonial bonds is much greater than that of whites. According to the 1932 statistics, there were only 1,720 colored marriages in comparison with 10,356 white. On the other hand there were nearly as many illegitimate births reported among the Negroes as among the whites, although the Negroes constitute less than a third of the population.

Pointing to these characteristics, a number of white Cubans are inclined to regard the Negro as mentally and morally inferior. It is not difficult, however, to explain these manifestations on economic, social and cultural grounds. The solution for the defects which have appeared to a greater extent in Negro than in white life must be sought not in a policy of repression but in improvement of social and economic environment.

These negative aspects of the Cuban Negro have been offset to a certain extent at least by the contributions which he has made to Cuban culture. Afro-Cuban music and dance have become internationally famous. Perhaps the leading musicians in Cuban history have been Negroes—Brindis de Salas, José White and José M. Jiménez—while one of its leading poets was the mulatto, Plácido. The Cuban colored population may eventually assist in the development of an art which will be as distinctive as Indian art in Mexico.

. . .

Race Prejudice

During the revolutions of 1868 and 1895 the white Cubans and Negroes were drawn closely together against Spain. In the latter revolution several leading Cuban generals were mulattoes, notably Antonio Maceo, and possibly a majority of the ordinary troops in the revolution were colored. The interracial fraternity which then existed was illustrated by the saying of Ignacio Agramonte concerning his mulatto servant, Ramón Agüero: "This is my brother." On numerous occasions José Martí declared that the fear entertained against the Negro race in Cuba was unjustified. "The Negro as such," he declared "is neither inferior nor superior to any other man. . . ." Because of this historic association and the general Latin attitude toward interracial relations, racial prejudice in Cuba has not been nearly so acute as in Anglo-Saxon countries. It seems true, however, that it has increased during the past few years. This is attributed partly to the unconscious influence of the American point of view and partly to economic distress. When an economic system is unable to provide adequately for the wants of every class in the population, the dominant group inevitably employs the racial argument to maintain its economic position at the expense of lesser colored groups.

Negroes, however, are freely admitted to the schools and University. Out of a total of 426,708 students, 105,586, or 24.6 percent, are colored, which is slightly less than the proportion which the Negroes bear to the total population. Large numbers of colored persons attend the normal schools—in Havana they constitute 80 percent of the total. Nevertheless, according to official figures, the number of colored teachers is only 1,181 out of a total of 7,417, or less than 19 percent—a number which probably is underestimated. At the same time, many Negro teachers have difficulty in being placed, partly because of lack of political influence. Although there are no legal discriminations against Negroes, custom decrees that in many parks and plazas the Negroes shall occupy a section apart from the whites. White and black students mix in the class rooms of the University, but hold their social functions apart. Colored people are not admitted to white clubs or *quintas*. At times they have been prohibited from bathing at certain public beaches, although such prohibition is illegal.

There are few Negro doctors, lawyers or intellectuals of standing in Cuba, nor are there many successful Negro business men. A recent statement of the *Comité por Los Derechos del Negro* declares:

> There are industries where they cannot work; in commerce, in the great foreign enterprises, above all,

> Negroes are not employed. In certain industries they work where the pay is least: for example, in the graphic arts they may be compositors, but seldom linotypists; in the tobacco industry they are cigar-makers and strippers, but not sorters or trimmers who are the employees that earn the best wages.

There is no adequate evidence to show whether this is due to lack of opportunity or aptitude.

Before the abolition of slavery, a number of slave revolts took place in Cuba. In 1907 an Independent Party of Color was organized, which supposedly started the 1912 revolution in which three thousand Negroes lost their lives. At the initiative of a Cuban Negro Senator, a law was passed in 1910, known after its author, as the Morúa law, which prohibited the formation of political parties on racial lines; this law is apparently still in force. Negroes have nevertheless played a role, if a subordinate one, in Cuba's politics. . . .

. . .

Following the downfall of Machado, fear of a Negro uprising again took hold of certain sections of the Cuban population. Having suffered perhaps even more severely than the whites in the recent depression, many Negroes naturally attempted to improve their economic position at a time when a wave of revolutionary sentiment swept the island. Negroes were among the leaders in seizing sugar properties and making exorbitant demands on mill managers. Moreover, following the revolt of the sergeants, the percentage of Negro officers and enlisted men in the Cuban army greatly increased. Although detailed statistics are not available, some estimates declare that today 35 percent of the enlisted men are Negroes. The social legislation of the Grau regime, combined with the policy of deporting Haitian Negroes, undoubtedly benefited the Cuban colored population. The Grau administration also appointed a number of Negroes to public office, including the first Negro judge. During the post-Machado period some Cuban Negroes attempted to abolish social discrimination. In January 1934 Negroes in Trinidad entered the section of the central park reserved by custom to the whites, declaring that there was nothing in the Cuban Constitution to justify segregation. As a result of this incident, rioting occurred, one Negro being killed.

These efforts of the Negro in the post-Machado period, which often took an extreme form, alarmed many conservative Cubans. In the past the politicians among the leading parties have been able to control the Negro vote by means of petty bribery and other inducements. But as a result of the unrest which has penetrated Cuban life, it is probable that the Cuban Negroes will be susceptible to new forms of political propaganda, and that with the growth of intelligent self-interest they will support movements which promise to improve their social and economic condition.

While racial prejudice against the Negro exists in certain white circles, this prejudice is not due to any inherent trait in the white race. The Cuban Negro exhibits a similar antipathy to the Haitian and Jamaican, whose standard of living and cultural level are considered lower than those of the Cuban colored class. Many Cuban Negro leaders sympathize with the deportation of Haitians inaugurated by the Grau regime. Racial prejudice also seems to exist between Negroes and mulattoes. For example, in Santiago de Cuba each group has its social club, from which members of the other group are excluded.

. . .

The Chinese

In the early part of the nineteenth century Chinese filtered into Cuba, coming originally from the Philippines via Spain. These Chinese were known as *Chinos Manilas.* Following the suppression of the Negro slave trade, the

Spanish government imported Chinese laborers under eight-year contracts, beginning in 1847. This type of importation continued intermittently until the conclusion of a treaty between China and Spain in October 1864, which defined the conditions of work of the Chinese laborers and provided that the laborer might purchase his discharge. Between 1853 and 1873 more than 132,000 Chinese were shipped to Cuba, 13 percent of whom died en route or shortly after their arrival. Chinese labor also complained of being grossly abused by employers, while Cubans declared that they committed many crimes, and did not have the vigor of the Negro.

Importation of Chinese came to an end in 1873. Five years later the Spanish government issued a decree requiring all Chinese whose contracts had terminated either to make a new contract or to leave the island, on the ground that many were criminals. In 1877 the Chinese population was reported to be about 44,000; by 1899 it totaled 14,863. Of this latter number only 49 were women.

In military order No. 155 of May 15, 1902 the American military government prohibited Chinese immigration into Cuba, with the exception of merchants and students. This order was enforced until 1919 when 1,100 entered, followed by 9,203 in 1920 and 1,858 in 1921. Apparently these admissions formed part of the Menocal policy of importing cheap labor from other areas, such as Haiti. In 1926 the Cuban government strengthened the prohibition against Chinese immigration by enacting Decree No. 570 which, with a few exceptions, admitted only Chinese diplomatic and consular representatives.

Between 1919 and 1931 the Chinese population increased from 10,300 to 24,480. The Chinese support several newspapers and a theatre in Havana and have clubs in many cities. In retail commerce, where they have gained a reputation for honesty, the Chinese offer severe competition to the Spaniards. During recent months a number of Chinese establishments have been bombed or threatened with bombing, presumably by disgruntled competitors. Other Chinese are employed in laundries, restaurants, or truck-gardening. Although only about five hundred marriages are reported between Chinese and Cubans, colored and white, the Chinese have left the mark of their blood throughout the island.

The Spanish Question

Despite the presence of a large Negro and a small Chinese minority, Cuba is predominantly Spanish in race and culture. Districts such as Holguín are very similar to Spain. The structure of the towns, type of architecture, the evening promenades in the plaza, life in the clubs, and even the small burros with milk cans dangling on each side are almost a replica of Spanish life.

Following its conquest of Cuba, the Spanish Crown carefully restricted the right of emigration to the West Indies. Despite the illicit entrance of numbers of Portuguese, Genevese and others, the Andalusians, belonging largely to military and bureaucratic classes, dominated immigration to Cuba. Beginning in the nineteenth century, however, the characteristics of this Spanish migration changed—Spaniards, who were accustomed to agricultural and commercial pursuits, now came from Asturias, Galicia, the Basque Provinces, Catalonia and the Canary Islands.

During the first two centuries the white population of the island was so scanty that Spain imposed the death penalty on any Castilian attempting to leave Cuba for America proper. When the British captured the Spanish colony of Jamaica in 1655, about eight thousand Spaniards fled to Cuba, while the slave insurrection in Haiti as well as the purchase of Louisiana by the United States caused an even greater number of Frenchmen to migrate there. The Spanish colony increased when Florida was ceded to the United States in 1819, and when the other Spanish colonies received their independence. As the last stronghold of Spain in the Western hemisphere, Cuba remained the military, agricultural and commercial center for many Spaniards.

At the beginning of the nineteenth century a distinction developed between the peninsular Spaniard, born in Spain—and the Cuban, the Spaniard born in Cuba. The former class came to Cuba to make a fortune or an official career; the Cuban had come to look on the island as a permanent home. The colonial policy accentuated this distinction by withholding from the Creoles, as the Cubans were called, privileges extended to Spaniards. In 1860 there were 513,000 Cubans in the island, divided almost equally between men and women. The Spaniards numbered 83,000, of whom 66,000 were men. At the end of the Spanish War the Cubans had increased to 1,466,633, while the Spaniards numbered 106,164. Today there are officially 614,000 Spaniards in Cuba, or 15.6 percent of the entire population—a figure which well-informed observers believe to be greatly exaggerated. There are about 75,000 more men than women in the Spanish colony, many of the men having married Cubans.

Although Spain was obliged to give up its political control over Cuba, the Treaty of Paris protected the private rights of Spaniards in the island. The Spanish colony has since been strengthened by a constant stream of immigration. Between 1903 and 1933, 723,381 Spaniards entered Cuba; of this number several hundred thousand have returned to Spain. In 1920 a record of 94,294 immigrants was made; following a decline during the next two years, the figure rose again to 46,439. As a result of the depression, however, the tide has swung in the other direction. In 1931 and 1932 more Spaniards returned to Spain than migrated to Cuba. In the former year only 1,210 Spaniards entered the country. Nevertheless, the Spanish colony remains large, and is distinct from the Cubans proper. In 1919 only 14 percent of the Spaniards were Cuban citizens, and the percentage probably remains unchanged.

For many years a number of Spaniards, especially from the Canary Islands, came to Cuba annually to work on the sugar crop and then returned to Spain. Belonging to the type of seasonal labor known as *golondrinas* or swallows, they lived together in primitive, coöperative units, dwelling in special *barracones* under the most unsanitary conditions. With the importation of Negroes from Haiti and Jamaica and the growth of the depression, this type of Spanish migration has come to an end.

15

INTERNATIONAL BANK FOR RECONSTRUCTION AND DEVELOPMENT

Policies and Attitudes of the Cuban Labor Movement

In 1950 the International Bank for Reconstruction and Development sent a team of experts to Cuba in order to investigate all aspects of the socio-economic scene and make recommendations for future development. The report of the Economic and Technical Mission stressed the role of private enterprise and the principles of "orthodox" economic policy. The Cuban government tried to implement some of the recommendations, but by 1959 many of the problems analyzed by the mission were still

---

From International Bank for Reconstruction and Development, *Report on Cuba: Findings and Recommendations of an Economic and Technical Mission Organized by the International Bank for Reconstruction and Development in Collaboration with the Government of Cuba in 1950* (Baltimore, Md., The Johns Hopkins Press, 1951), pp. 364–366, 371–372. Reprinted by permission of the International Bank for Reconstruction and Development.

unsolved. The following conclusion of the group then emerged as a fulfilled prophecy:

> Failure to choose the dynamic alternative can bring to Cuba consequences of the utmost seriousness. . . . If leaders have neglected to prepare Cuba for this, they will be held to blame by the people. And, if that should happen, control may well pass into subversive but specious hands—as it has done in other countries whose leaders have ignored the trends of the times.

The prevalent pattern of trade-union organization is that of local unions, covering employees of each establishment or enterprise, linked into federations of the union in the same industry or similar industries. The Cuban Confederation of Labor (CTC) unites most of these federations. There are also some independent unions and a rival General Confederation of Labor (CGT).

The union-organized sectors of the Cuban economy include the extremely important sugar industry, in which the agricultural workers as well as the workers in the mills and offices are unionized; practically all of manufacturing industry; transportation (railroads, port operations, busses, etc.); communications; electric power, hotel and restaurant operations; banking; and some of the larger retail stores.

Union organization is weak or nonexistent in the multitude of smaller commercial enterprises which together comprise an important segment of the Cuban economy; in cattle-raising; in coffee-growing; and on small farms other than those attached to the sugar industry.

Altogether, the CTC claims 800,000 members and

the outside unions several hundred thousand more. Well-informed observers, however, regard these claims as highly inflated, and there are not authentic figures based on anything like an audited, dues-paying membership count.

A weakness of Cuban unions is the wide gap which often exists between the leadership and the rank and file. Membership is too frequently more nominal than real (in the sense of active, informed participation). The standard of education of the members is generally low. Cuban unions, for the most part, lack a really strong democratic base, and they are not firmly founded in legitimate collective bargaining relations at the factory and shop level.

They tend, therefore, to become sounding-boards for ambitious political leaders who seek to advance some doctrine or party in the name of organized labor or to promote their personal fortunes and positions in politics.

This is not to indict all union leaders. There are those who deplore these weaknesses in the movement and would like to correct them. But the fundamental problem is to improve the education and sense of democratic responsibility of the rank and file. This must take time, even when something is being done about it. Little, however, is being done today by the public educational system, by the unions, or by employers, though all three certainly have a stake in the problem.

In the colonial days, labor leadership in Cuba came largely from anarcho-syndicalists of the Bakunin school. A strong thread of their ideology, with its emphasis on "direct action," its contempt for legality, and its denial that there can be common interests of worker and employers, persists in the Cuban labor movement in modern times. Machado, in the twenties, smashed the anarcho-syndicalist leadership.

A new Communist leadership thereupon arose. Until 1933 it was clandestine. Subsequently, the Communist leaders worked in the open at times, were suppressed at times, and at times worked in political alliance with the government.

From 1933 to 1947 the Communists, by superior industriousness, devotion, training, and tactical skill—all of which qualities their bitterest enemies emphasized—succeeded in attaining practically complete control of the Cuban labor movement. In late 1947 control of the CTC was wrested from them, and with the help of the government was lodged in the hands of leaders affiliated with the "*Auténtico*" or Government party, where it remains today.

In the fall of 1950, while the Mission was in Cuba, the Communist daily newspaper in Havana, *Hoy,* was suppressed by the Government. Communists, however, still have a strong underground influence in some unions, and some authorities estimate that perhaps 25 percent of all Cuban workers are secretly sympathetic to them.

The new leaders are, in some respects, less skillful and experienced in trade union matters than the Communists whom they displaced. Because of their close connections, too, with the Government party many regard them primarily as political rather than labor leaders. Hence, they are under constant pressure to demonstrate to the rank and file that they can "deliver" more for the worker and can carry on a "struggle" with employers even more uncompromising than that of the former leaders.

Finally, it must be remembered that nearly all the popular education of working people on how an economic system works and what might be done to improve it came first from the anarcho-syndicalists, and most recently—and most effectively—from the Communists.

. . .

Perhaps the most significant theme which emerged in these interviews might be called "lack of confidence."

Several different labor leaders were asked about union policies which restrict production and productivity. They replied that they realized that it would be better for everyone if there could be higher production, expanding industries, and new job opportunities. They had no confidence, however, that Cuban employers and investors would show the necessary initiative and enterprise, even if labor did make concessions.

On the contrary, they asserted that gains from concessions by labor would not be used constructively. The increased productivity would go to increase already large profits. It would be absorbed by the propensity of Cuban businessmen to exact an excessive profit per unit while keeping volume of output low.

This, it will be noted, is the converse of the "lack of confidence" on the part of Cuban investors—described elsewhere—which stems, in no small part, from the attitudes and policies of organized labor. In both cases, no doubt the reasons given are partly real and partly excuses. But, in both cases, this lack of confidence harms the Cuban economy.

One labor spokesman explained the attitude of his union towards a more efficient method which is much feared in case it reduce the number of jobs:

This attitude, he said, must be viewed against the background of a country in which the employer class consists largely of inactive owners—grasping and commercially minded—and in which population growth is not matched by the growth of new industries.

Any savings in cost from this technical improvement, he maintained, would not accrue to the Cuban working people, but to the employers in the industry and to the merchants. This union therefore was not willing to see its men displaced in order to increase the merchants' profits.

Another labor leader, speaking of a similar problem in another line of work, said:

"As long as the labor movement cannot be certain that the money saved would be invested productively there is no reason why we should make the sacrifice."

. . .

Labor spokesmen frequently referred to the effects of the former treatment of workers by employers and the state. They said that these memories are still active and induce sentiments—particularly among the less-educated rank and file—which make it difficult for the leaders to follow constructive and rational policies. The continued influence of these past abuses makes itself felt in policies which are emotional and antagonistic.

One leader, who seemed particularly thoughtful and frank, was inclined to admit the truth of a number of the complaints of employers, but insisted repeatedly that all these problems had to be viewed in the perspective of the very recent change in labor's position.

Organized labor, he said, does seem unreasonable in its attitude at times. But that comes from history. Not so long ago, the mill owner had power almost of life and death over the workers. If a worker got in the bad graces of a mill owner the latter might call up the rural military guard and say, "whip this man," or even "hang him," and they would do it.

The sentiment among many workers today, he explained, is something like revenge. But the labor movement should try to come down to facts. It should be willing to talk special concessions to encourage new industries, and so on. But in Cuba the hot-blooded attitude is a factor.

Managers, he continued, with some outstanding exceptions, are reluctant to talk things over with the union. They still try to reject the union. Many workers still think in terms of fighting the employers. With time they should be able to come together. But the change from the old times is so recent that labor still remembers and hates.

16

BORIS S. NIKIROV

Communism and the Struggle for Power Within the Labor Movement

The labor movement in Cuba has had a long tradition of radical orientation. Anarcho-syndicalist influence was important from the 1890's to the late 1920's, when the Communists began to claim the mantle of radical leadership. This latter development culminated in 1939 when the new labor federation, the Confederation of Cuban Workers (CTC), was organized under Communist influence.

During the latter 1940's a pitched battle was waged for control of the labor movement between the labor group of the Auténtico party (which had been formed in the early 1930's by Trotskyites) and the Communists. The newly victorious Auténtico party wanted the political leverage offered by control of the CTC (the Communists had been

---

Translated from Boris S. Nikirov, "Iz Istorii Rabochego Dvizheniia na Kube" ("From the History of the Labor Movement in Cuba"), *Voprosy Istorii*, 9 (September, 1961), 103–115.

aligned with the Batista forces), and this was probably a more important factor in the struggle than ideology.

This analysis by Boris S. Nikirov, a faculty member at Moscow University, is a generally accurate presentation of the "other side" of the controversy. The interpretation of these events is highly influenced by the author's point of view; but the same thing can be said about almost everything which has been written on this controversy. This article is indicative of the Russian interest in Cuban and Latin American studies which has been growing especially since 1960. It is also an example of how the Russian scholars are interpreting Cuban developments within the framework of Russian historical patterns, just as United States scholars have done in the past with their own historical patterns.

At the end of the thirties, on the initiative and with the participation of the Communist party of Cuba, a united, democratic, trade union organization was founded, the Confederation of Cuban Workers (CTC). It joined together the largest trade-union organizations in the country: the unions of workers in the sugar industry, tobacco workers, dock workers, railroad workers, etc. The most important moment in the class struggle of the Cuban workers was the defense of trade-union unity as a necessary condition for maintaining the fighting capacity of the labor movement in its struggle against capitalist exploitation and the schemes of imperialist agents. In the present article we will examine several questions in the struggle of the Cuban laborers for the maintenance of the CTC in the years 1944–1948.

. . .

At the head of all the progressive forces in the country stood the Communist Party of Cuba, which was founded in 1925. In 1944 the party changed its name and began to be called the Popular Socialist Party of Cuba (PSP). During World War II the PSP grew into a huge force which had great influence on the progressive trade-union organizations of the country and on the Confederation of Cuban Workers. The party actively participated in politics. It had representatives in the Chamber of Deputies and in the Senate.

. . .

The democratic trade-union movement in Cuba grew stronger during the war. The main mass of workers was collected around the Confederation of Cuban Workers, which included workers belonging to the most diverse political parties: Communists, Auténticos, Republicans, etc.

The democratic leadership of the executive committee of the CTC came out for the unification of the trade-union movement in the country, figuring that the CTC ought to unite all the workers without regard to their political affiliations. In the fall of 1944, the CTC proposed to the Auténticos—who had created a special apparatus for leading the union movement, the Labor Commission—that they join with the CTC. This proposal was accepted and the leaders of the Labor Commission became part of the executive committee of the CTC. Into the CTC also came a few so-called neutral trade unions. The united front of the trade-union movement under the leadership of the CTC, despite its fragility and the constant efforts of the Labor Commission to destroy this unity, brought a valuable contribution to the labor movement in Cuba.

The Cuban workers well understood the importance of trade-union unity. It more than once helped them successfully repel attacks of the entrepreneurs and their agents, which were aimed at lowering the living standard of the workers. Trade-union unity paralyzed attempts by the reaction to destroy the democratic labor movement.

As a consequence, when they came to power, the Auténticos, with the help of the government apparatus now in their hands, bent all efforts toward gaining leadership of the CTC and destroying trade-union unity of the Cuban workers.

The period 1944–1948 was one of stormy militant activity for the Cuban working class.

During World War II, the CTC had achieved certain successes in the struggle to improve the condition of the working class. A minimum wage was established for workers in the leading professions. The CTC had been officially recognized by the government and gained the right, along with representatives of the government and industry, to take part in the annual negotiations with the U.S. on the sale of sugar. . . . The industrialists had to agree to a payment to the workers at the end of the year, a remuneration (the so-called differential), in case there was a rise in sugar prices.

. . .

The growing influence of the CTC and the democratic trade-union movement bothered the American monopolists and their Cuban agents more and more. At the end of 1945, the American Federation of Labor (AFL) increased its subversive activity in Cuba. For many years it had been an agent of the imperialists in the labor movement, attempting to divide the trade-union movement of Latin America and dominate it. Even before World War II, the AFL had tried to create a "yellow" grouping of unions of Latin America, the so-called Pan-American Labor Conference. But this venture did not succeed. . . . With the aim of splitting the Cuban trade-union movement, the AFL held a special meeting in Miami (Florida) from the twenty-third to the thirty-first of January, 1946, concerning the struggle with the democratic trade-union movement in Latin America headed by the CTLA. Illegally present at this meeting were the leaders of the Auténticos' Labor Commission, J. Arévalo and F. Aguirre (members of the CTC executive committee) who had even earlier held secret conversations with Green and other leaders of the AFL on a co-operative campaign against the CTC. In Miami Arévalo and Aguirre discussed with the AFL leaders the means by which the Labor Commission could take over the leadership of the CTC.

After discovering the separatist and predatory activities of Arévalo and Aguirre, the executive committee called them to account. At a session of the National Council of the CTC the dissenters were unmasked and censured. Arévalo and Aguirre were forced to repent and to pledge their loyalty to the unity of the trade-union movement of the country. But this was only a tactical maneuver to which the Labor Commission leaders resorted because the dissenters did not have enough strength in the trade unions to wage an open struggle with the CTC and its democratic leadership. Soon they were to undertake a new maneuver to split the trade union movement.

Attempting to take the leadership of the CTC into their own hands, the leaders of the Labor Commission proposed a change in the structure of the Confederation's executive committee: instead of a general secretary, the CTC should create a secretariat of five members, in which the dissenters demanded three places for themselves (E. Mujal, F. Aguirre, J. Arévalo). The executive committee refused to reorganize behind the back of the National Congress of the Confederation. According to the statutes only the National Congress could change the structure of the executive committee which it had created. This attempt of the Auténticos to take the leadership of the CTC into their hands failed.

The culminating point in the struggle for leadership of the country's trade-union movement was the period of preparing for and holding the Fifth National Congress of the CTC.

. . .

As a counter to the Fifth Congress of the CTC the dissenters organized their "congress of trade unions" which opened on July 6, 1947, in Panama under Mujal's chairmanship. The names of the delegates were not reported. Plain-clothes police and soldiers were sitting in the hall of the convention. . . .

On July 30, 1947, on the basis of oral instructions from the Minister of Labor, Prío Socarrás, police occupied the CTC's Palace of Labor, which had been built by workers' subscriptions and which had long served as resident headquarters of the Confederation of Cuban Workers. The CTC strongly protested to the President of the republic and demanded repeal of the labor minister's orders. Besides that, the leaders of the CTC submitted an official complaint against the action of Socarrás in the Havana City Court. However, the CTC's protests against this illegal seizure of the premises were fruitless. The government announced the transfer of the Palace of Labor to the puppet CTC with A. Cofiño at its head. In answer to this decision by the government, strikes of protest broke out all over the country.

The seizure of the Palace of Labor represented the start of a widespread government take-over of the holdings of trade-union organizations which supported the CTC. . . .

. . .

On October 11, 1947, the Ministry of Labor published a decree declaring the Confederation of Cuban Workers outside the law and transferring all its legal rights to the government-controlled puppet CTC.

On October 13, 1947, the workers of the country met this act with a general strike. The government threw police and troops against the strikers. More than a thousand persons were arrested. . . .

The strike was supported by trade unions of other countries. Thus, the furriers' union, part of the CIO, protested to President Grau San Martín against the repression of the CTC, demanded repeal of the anti-labor laws and the release of the arrested members of the trade unions.

. . .

The inability of the Auténticos to destroy the democratic trade unions of Cuba made the American monopolies reigning in Cuba lose faith in them. In 1948 General Batista, who had arrived from the United States, again appeared in the Cuban political arena. Monopolies again put their stakes on an open military dictatorship. Batista, with money at his disposal, revived the intense political activity, grouping around himself the most reactionary elements. In 1952, after overthrowing the government of Prío Socarrás . . . , Batista established a military dictatorship in the country.

For the seven-year period of Batista's dictatorship . . . the working class and the democratic trade-union movement of Cuba suffered heavy losses. The Popular-Socialist party, the avant-garde of the Cuban working class, was prohibited and suppressed. Hundreds and thousands of trade-union activists were thrown into prison, tortured, and shot. The Confederation of Cuban Workers, forbidden by the authorities, was subjected to extremely cruel repression. The "yellow" CTC, with Mujal, the former leader of the Auténticos' "Labor Commission," at its head and created on the orders of the AFL, actively co-operated with Batista's dictatorship. . . .

17

WILLIAM S. STOKES

National and Local Violence in Cuban Politics

Gang warfare and other types of violence are symptoms of social problems and prevailing attitudes about the nature of politics. Cuba in the 1940's and 1950's was the scene of much armed conflict as numerous groups tried to gain status or protect their position. By the latter part of the 1950's much of this conflict had been channeled into the struggle to overthrow the Batista government. In the process, some of the private armies which had been formed (such as Senator Rolando Masferrer's force) devoted their energies to protecting the regime.

Professor William S. Stokes believes that the widespread use of violence derives in large part from various conditioning elements in the Cuban culture, and that all this is related to an endemic, authoritarian outlook. This view provides a distinct

From William S. Stokes, "National and Local Violence in Cuban Politics," *The Southwestern Social Science Quarterly,* XXXIV, 3, (September, 1953), 57–63. Reprinted by permission of the publisher.

challenge to those who maintain that pre-1959 Cubans were strongly oriented to the democratic approach.

Professor Stokes is one of the leading experts in the field of Latin American government, and has served on the political science faculty at the University of Wisconsin. He is currently at Pomona College, California.

II

Although there does not seem to be much interest among American scholars in the problem of mobilizing power in Latin American politics, it is evident that there is wide understanding in the United States of the existence of forceful methods of organizing and changing governments at the national level. What is not so generally known is that the pattern of violence can frequently be found at other levels as well. For the purpose of this brief study, permit me to examine the extent to which violence was employed for political purposes in urban politics in Cuba for 1949–50.

Organized use of force in urban areas in Cuba is seen primarily in connection with the party factions, the university, terrorist groups, and the labor unions. The University of Havana, for example, is one of the principal sources of political power in Cuban politics, and both students and faculty are active participants in practices that frequently are violent. The year 1949 began with the assassination of two students, supposedly for having participated in the shooting of a police sergeant, who in turn reputedly took part in the shooting of Manolo Castro, President of the Havana University Student Federation. In February, the sessions of the Faculty of the Social Sciences were interrupted by a fusillade of revolver shots. On April 2, assassins riddled Justo Fuentes, Vice-president of the University Student Federation, in front of the COCO broadcasting station. The activities of the *bonches* (terrorist gangs) became so conspicuous during the year that *El Mundo* (large liberal daily in Havana) declared editorially:

> . . . violence holds sway in the halls of the University. Professors and students are nothing but the prisoners of a few groups of desperadoes, who impose their will and whim and pass their examinations at pistol point. The University Council itself has declared its powerlessness to repress these gangs for lack of means of coercion.

Early in September some two hundred police officers violated the autonomy of the university (the university has traditionally been regarded as neutral ground in violent struggles for power in politics) by invading the School of Agronomy and arresting fourteen persons. The police confiscated a large cache of armament which included machine guns, rifles, revolvers, and thousands of bullets. The struggle for control of student offices in the university and for the spoils of government in the capital continued. On September 20, Gustavo Mejías, President of the School of Sciences Student Association, was shot to death at the university bathing establishment at Marianao, apparently in a conflict over control over the funds and proceeds of the bar. Following the assassination of the student Nestor Múñoz Giral and the wounding of Julia Dupín Palacios on the third floor of the Havana Institute, the Ministry of Education in January, 1950, suspended classes, closed the institute's student association, deposed its leaders, and seized its headquarters and property.

The major revolutionary organizations employing assassination, small-scale attacks with weapons up to machine guns, and the use of bombs and dynamite include UIR (Unión Insurreccional Revolucionaria), MSR (Movimiento Socialista Revolucionario), and ARG (Acción Revolucionaria Guiteras). In 1948, when I was last in Cuba on a research mission, the chiefs of UIR were alleged to be Jinjaume and Diegues; Comandante Ignacio Mendieta and Lieutenant Armando Correa of the police were mentioned as members; and known terrorists such as Miguel Múñoz, Miguel de la Cámara, and Oramas Roque were included. The former leader of the UIR, Major Emilio Tró, director of the National Police Academy, was killed in 1947 in a mass gang fight in which the opposition was led by Major Mario Salabarría, head of the police Bureau of Investigation and Special Information. Major Antonio Morín Dopico, former police chief of the town of Marianao, lost his life in the same street battle.

The MSR had received considerable public notice in recent years for its "direct action" tactics. Orlando Masferrer, congressman representing the Republican party, is generally recognized as its major leader in government. The police stopped Congressman Masferrer and three of his friends on the evening of December 18, 1948, and found that one of the party was armed with a .45-caliber submachine gun and the other three had .38 revolvers. Various attempts have been made by the rival terrorist groups to liquidate Masferrer. As he was leaving the Capitol on September 15, 1949, the occupants of two cars which had been slowly cruising in the vicinity opened fire and killed one pedestrian and wounded several others. Masferrer escaped unscathed.

Perhaps the most notorious of the *pistoleros* of the MSR are Orlando León Lemús ("El Colorado") and Policarpo Soler, whose many acts of violence forced them underground. Police Chief Colonel José M. Caramés declared that these *pistoleros* were protected by members of the government. The MSR was involved in spectacular violence in the summer of 1950.

At about eleven o'clock one evening, an Oldsmobile drove slowly past the house of José de Jinjaume, leader of UIR. As it passed, its occupants fired their weapons and in that way decoyed the occupants of the house into rushing into the street, at which time a Plymouth which was following spurted into view. The men inside opened up with machine guns, killing José A. Rodríguez Cremet and José Carreras Albelo and wounding Armando Correa, José Antonio Zarranz, Juan Cancio de la Rosa, and Mario Martínez. Jinjaume escaped without a wound. Congressman Masferrer's chauffeur, Carlos Alonso Jiménez ("Tronco de Yuca")was arraigned on July 28, 1950, on charges of participating in the attack.

The ARG was originally linked with the government of the Revolution, which obtained power after the 1933 debacle, with Ramón Grau San Martín (1944–48), and continued with Carlos Prío Socarrás (1948–52). The ARG came into the spotlight in October 1940, when Narciso ("Chicho") Rodríguez Guerra, secretary general of the municipal and provincial section of the Auténtico party, the then governing party, was shot fourteen times by six men. Four men, active members of the ARG, were apprehended in the home of Mario Antonio Hirigoyen, secretary general of the labor union of Autobuses Modernos and himself a leader in the ARG, and were charged with the offense. The four were Juan Solís Cabrera, Francisco Lazo Fernández, Hugo Parra Velazco, and Nivaldo Noriega Borgés ("El Niño").

Other manifestations of violence in urban politics in very recent times in Cuba include these incidents: the forceful entry into the Havana Court House in July, 1950, and seizure of the records which the government was using to prosecute former President Ramón Grau San Martín on charges of allegedly misappropriating $174,000,000 of public funds; assassinations—Communist port-labor leader Aracelio Iglesias, October, 1948; Rubén Darío González, January, 1949; José Ramón Solís and Roberto Enríquez López, July, 1949; Guillermo Salazar ("Wichy") and Francisco Fernández Cristóbal ("El Flaco"), September, 1949; Congressman Carlos Fraile Goldarás, May, 1950; and Undersecretary of the

Treasury Dr. Tulio Paniagua, October, 1950; bombings —Ministry of Labor, December, 1948; Ministry of Wealth, December, 1948; home of former Minister of Education, Miguel A. de la Guardia, January, 1949; Provincial Government building, January, 1949; and finally, repeated threats to use force on the part of major groups in politics, such as the powerful National Federation of Sugar Workers which declared that their revolutionary commandos were ready to fight their enemies, including the Rural Guard.

III

It should be remembered that the evidence here presented demonstrates only that the *cuartelazo* of March 10, 1952, has its parallel in urban violence concerned with political objectives short of supreme power. Although the illustrations of urban violence are selected for the time period 1949–50 and are related primarily to Havana, Cuba's capital and largest city, my research has led me to the conclusion that any other year or years could have been selected with similar results found. Indeed, without verifying this statement by quantitative comparison, it seems fair to me to say that the incidence of violence for political purposes was as great during the administrations of Ramón Grau San Martín and Carlos Prío Socarrás (1944–48 and 1948–52 respectively) as for any other period in Cuba's history. The evidence appears conclusive to me that violence in Cuban politics is not confined to an occasional change of power at the national level but is instead characteristic of politics at all levels and in both urban and rural areas.

If this generalization can be accepted, then it follows that violence in politics is more than an accidental, haphazard occurrence. It is logical to suppose that force is a technique for mobilizing political power and organizing and changing governments which has a long history and is a fundamental part of the thinking of Cuban citizens interested in government and politics. The illustrations of the employment of violence for purposes other than organizing power at the national level suggest that force is also used to influence the appointment of personnel, the formulation of policy, and the adjudication of competing interests. This does not necessarily mean that Cubans prefer the methodology of violence to that of election of the liberal-democratic state. It does mean that Cubans in the cities and in the country, in the rich and poor classes, in the university and in the labor unions, all are willing to employ violence for both national and local political purposes.

. . .

. . . It is my own hypothesis that force and violence in organizing, maintaining, and changing government derive from the conditioning influence of such social organizations as the family, church, educational facilities, army, and economic system. These social organizations, although influenced profoundly by the liberal-democratic institutions of the United States, nevertheless still tend to be more authoritarian in the Iberian tradition than democratic in the Anglo-American tradition. . . .

18

FEDERICO G. GIL

❋

Cuban Politics and Political Parties: 1933-1953

The decade following World War II was a crucial one for the hopes of democratic government in Cuba, but the elements of political democracy which had been emerging since 1940 were rudely aborted by Fulgencio Batista's "golpe de estado" of March, 1952. In the following selection Federico Gil, Professor of Political Science at the University of North Carolina, analyzes these political developments which helped to set the stage for the struggle to overthrow Batista.

Professor Gil has written extensively on Latin American politics and government, and is currently director of the Institute of Latin American Studies at the University of North Carolina.

From Federico G. Gil, "Antecedents of the Cuban Revolution," *The Centennial Review of Arts and Science,* VI, No. 3 (Summer, 1962), 376–382. Reprinted by permission of the publisher and of the author.

After 1933, Cuban politics focused upon two figures who emerged from the revolutionary process. One was a civilian, the physician Ramón Grau San Martín, destined to be the leader of the so-called Authentic Revolution. The other, a young sergeant, Fulgencio Batista, rose from poverty to the position of strong-man and president-maker, becoming the symbol and guarantor of stability and public order against revolutionary excesses. After starting at a brisk pace during the "pentarchy" government (September 4–10, 1933), the revolution took further steps forward during the provisional presidency of Grau San Martín (September 10, 1933–January 17, 1934), and then came almost to a standstill. The refusal of the United States to recognize Grau San Martín was an important factor in the fall of his government. Concerned with the dangers inherent in social revolution and its impact on U.S. vested interests in the island, American policy was aimed at preservation of the status quo.

Sumner Welles and later Jefferson Caffery, as personal representatives of President Roosevelt, played a major role in bringing the revolution to a halt. From then on, the revolution became chiefly political, not social and economic. One cannot help but wonder whether or not events in Cuba would have taken a different course, if the United States at that time had favored needed social and economic changes in Latin America as it is doing now. It is valid to pose such a question, for in some respects the Cuban phenomenon of the 1950's was simply the reincarnation of the revolutionary process interrupted in the 1930's. Set in motion again, this process was to lead, in our time, to disastrous consequences in Cuban-American relations. Also, this time, the Revolution was to become chiefly social and economic, not political.

Gradually, Batista, the one-time sergeant, emerged as the arbiter of Cuba's destiny. Until 1940, he ruled through puppet presidents, seven in all, among whom

Carlos Mendieta (January, 1934–December, 1936), Miguel Mariano Gómez (1936), and Federico Laredo Brú (1936–1940) were the chief incumbents. Without ever disowning the revolutionary creed, Batista veered to a more conservative course, thus bringing recognition from the United States and the support of foreign investors and the great vested interests. He ruled sternly from behind the presidential chair with the backing of the army until 1940 when he officially assumed the chief executive's office, securing election with the support of a coalition of parties which included the political machines which had once dominated Cuban politics and supported dictator Machado.

For seven years, the constitutional basis of the Cuban government had remained irregular, but on October 10, 1940, a new constitution was adopted. Many of the provisions of this constitution represented radical departures from tradition and reflected the interest in social reform. Despite all the vicissitudes of the post-revolutionary period, the new basic law was clearly the fruit of the Revolution, reflecting the influence of all those who advocated political, economic, and social changes. It was thought at the time that, at least, the trials and tribulations of the preceding decade had not all been in vain.

Meanwhile, the repository of the ideals of the revolution of 1933 had become the PRC or Cuban Revolutionary Party (Auténtico), founded in 1934 as a number of revolutionary organizations combined forces. The PRC played a leading role in drafting the Constitution of 1940, and was to win the presidency in 1944 and 1948. Its program featured economic and political nationalism and social justice while committing the PRC to fundamental reforms. It favored government control of the sugar industry, the establishment of a tribunal of accounts and a national bank, a budget law, tax reforms, a civil service, creation of a merchant marine, the expansion of education, etc. It also emphasized probity in administration. Under the colorful leadership of Dr. Grau San Martín, who gained immense popularity as the Batista regime became more and more corrupt in the midst of a new bonanza brought about by steady sugar prices, the PRC gained power through a sweeping electoral victory in 1944. It remained in office until the military coup of 1952. In 1948, although somewhat weaker than in 1944, the PRC's candidate Carlos Prío Socarrás handily won the election.

During its two terms in power, the PRC carried out a considerable part of its program with some success. It was a firm exponent of political democracy and it maintained scrupulous respect for civil liberties. It established a well-designed policy of stabilization of the price of sugar and of better distribution of the wealth derived from this product; it sought to reduce the dangers of a one-crop economy, gave impulse to a social security system, and generously financed a vast educational program. During the Prío Socarrás administration, important institutional reforms were undertaken and the Tribunal of Accounts and the National Bank were established. On the other hand, the PRC failed to achieve important measures it had promised, chiefly, agrarian reform. More importantly, far from responding to the popular clamor for honest and efficient government, the PRC immersed itself in graft and corruption on a scale surpassed only in recent years by Batista's second regime. The public became thoroughly disillusioned and bitter, and Grau San Martín was generally charged with the crime of perpetrating a cynical fraud upon the Cuban people through failure to implement and practice the very principles which he professed. The Auténticos had come to power with the most enthusiastic public support and with the high hopes of the people that it would accomplish the long-desired social reforms and a "purification" of governmental practices. These hopes came to naught after the Auténticos enjoyed two terms in possession of the presidency.

This situation was party responsible for the rise of a new and powerful organization, the Party of the Cuban People (Ortodoxo), an offshoot of the PRC, in 1946. By 1951, this party had become a formidable political force under the dynamic leadership of Eduardo Chibás who now became the standard-bearer of the campaign for honest government. The party program of "economic independence, political liberty, and social justice" included also an insistence on keeping the party free from political pacts. Much prestige had been lost by the PRC because of its disposition to ally itself with some of the old, traditional political groups. Observers agree that, despite the absence of Chibás, who committed suicide in 1951, had the election of 1952 not been prevented by the military coup, the Ortodoxos would have readily won the contest.

However, as this election approached, the political balance sheet showed a substantial margin on the credit side of the ledger: since 1940, the electoral processes, although not altogether free from marring vices, had been generally fair and honest. Batista himself had permitted an honest election in 1944 and had accepted with grace the victory of his arch-rival Grau San Martín over his own candidate. The Auténticos' victory in 1948 had been a clean one. Under such conditions there were grounds for hoping that, under the pressure of an electorate which had steadily grown more alert and articulate, and with the effectiveness of suffrage relatively assured, the return of morality in public office could eventually be attained. The best evidence that Cuba was an emergent democracy existed in the fact that the fullest freedom of expression and criticism was afforded the individual. Nevertheless, large segments of the population still longed for fundamental reforms of various institutions, and the bankrupt leadership had caused great disillusionment.

Cuban public opinion desperately desired the Revolution—"to mean, at least, a fundamental departure from the venality, corruption, and fraud so characteristic of

Cuban colonial and republican politics." This was demonstrated by the enthusiasm which Eduardo Chibás aroused by his passionate campaign for rectitude and integrity. And along with this went the conviction that these goals could be attained by democratic means. Meanwhile the country, in spite of thievery in public office and periodic looting of the treasury, had gone economically forward by leaps and bounds in a process of development only short of spectacular. There existed a strong organized labor movement, and some progress had been achieved toward social justice.

On March 10, 1952, eighty days before the scheduled elections, Batista, again a presidential candidate but without prospects of success, turned the clock back by his garrison revolt. This was the first, and in a sense, the greatest of his many crimes. What had come to be inconceivable in the minds of Cubans, namely, the settling of political contests by bayonets, suddenly became a frightful reality. Batista's only justification for his act was the woeful state into which public administration had fallen and the prevalence of political gangsterism. He obviously counted heavily upon public approval of what he was to do. The Ortodoxos had heaped such vilification upon the Prío Socarrás regime that Batista believed the people would welcome a change, even by violent means. Thus, although criticisms of Prío's regime were certainly well-founded, the highly charged, emotional temper of Cuban politics which led the Ortodoxo opposition to excessive abuses, contributed to undermine not only the administration but the institutional order as well. Responsibility for the debacle was also to fall in part upon the shoulders of President Prío Socarrás, whose inexplicable weakness in vacillating for hours before taking decisive action also contributed to the success of the coup. A close associate of Prío and prominent member of his government told me in 1952 of the astounding spectacle of the president sunk in a chair in an apparent stupor while telephones rang ceaselessly and delegations from political organizations and citizen groups flooded into his office. He was seemingly powerless from shock and helpless to react to the situation. The telephone calls were from chiefs of garrisons from all over the country seeking instructions (they had not yet gone over to Batista's side), and the delegations pouring into the palace were offering to take up arms.

Public opinion was dazed and a sensation of temporary paralysis invaded the entire nation. The usurping government interpreted this as acquiescence and Batista conceived the hope that it would be possible for him to consolidate his position rapidly by rebuilding his political machine, and, with an ad hoc electoral system, give legality to his government. This would be in line with the thinking of Batista, since those who know him well state that he is not a man of extremes, and only reverts to excesses when forced to do so. He had never achieved the one thing he has always wanted most, popularity. His failure can be traced in part to political circumstances, to his insatiable greed for wealth and power, and also to the methods he used to further his political career. This contention is well supported by the obvious vacillations between respect for legality and arbitrariness which characterized his rule.

However, public opinion reacted unfavorably to these events. In keeping with tradition, the University students soon assumed the vanguard of the opposition forces. Their ranks were swelled by the Ortodoxo and Auténtico parties in an attitude of passive resistance with some attempts at conspiratorial activity. It is not within the scope of this article to trace the events which finally led to the outbreak of a full-fledged revolution, but it may be well to summarize some of the major incidents in this process.

After restoring the Constitution of 1940, in response to public pressure, Batista decided to hold elections on November 3, 1953. Far from giving guarantees for the holding of such a contest, he imposed the Draconian legislation known as the *Ley de Orden Público*. On the eve of the elections the atmosphere of violence and coercion forced the withdrawal of the only candidate opposing Batista, Dr. Grau San Martín. So scandalous were these elections that even some of the partisans of Batista, whose personal ambitions had been thwarted, denounced them as a farce. The net result of the event was an increase of general agitation followed by a repression on the part of the government. The regime resorted to the creation of an unscrupulous and complex police apparatus employing a variety of violent methods and the jails filled rapidly with political prisoners. The opposition remained disunited and the two main political parties (Ortodoxos and Auténticos) were rent asunder by internal fragmentation.

III

❁ ❁ ❁

INTERPRETATIONS OF SOCIAL AND ECONOMIC DEVELOPMENT

19

ROLAND T. ELY

Cuba Emerges from Isolation: Economic and Social Changes Between 1760 and 1839

After a brief period of activity in the sixteenth century Cuba became something of a backwater of the Spanish Empire. The conquistadors sought El Dorado on the American continent, and in the process the island entered an era of imperial neglect. By the middle of the eighteenth century a distinctive culture had developed, characterized by widespread ownership of land and an emerging intellectual and artistic tradition. Important developments began during the latter half of the eighteenth century which, in the words of Ramiro Guerra, "created new living and working conditions that would soon complete the formation of our national identity."[1]

From Roland T. Ely, *Cuando Reinaba su Majestad el Azucar* (Buenos Aires, Editorial Sudamerica, 1963), pp. 87–88, 91–92, 101–103, 105–115. Reprinted by permission of the author.

[1] Ramiro Guerra y Sánchez, *Sugar and Society in the Caribbean*, New Haven, p. 43.

Professor Ely's discussion of this era illuminates not only the development of these new conditions but also the factors which revived an intense Spanish interest in Cuba. The peculiar impact on the island of the revolutions in other parts of the Spanish Empire is especially significant for any understanding of the social and political problems of the nineteenth century.

For any given half-century between 1760 and 1839, the expansion of Cuba's foreign commerce seems scarcely short of the miraculous. During the entire period, royal revenues—and they were largely dependent upon Customs House receipts—multiplied more than fifty times over. The story of Matanzas, some fifty miles to the eastward of Havana, offers an interesting case in point. An insignificant little fishing village for most of the eighteenth century (in 1762, for instance, it provided exactly $74 in revenue to the royal exchequer), by 1818 this settlement had grown into a bustling seaport. In the latter year, Matanzas poured over one quarter of a million dollars into the Cuban Treasury. Much of the impetus to the growth of this coastal hamlet came from European capitalists who had been unable to return to the Peninsula, when it was invaded by French armies. Having established new plantations and commercial houses, they ". . . decided to remain on the Island of Cuba and especially in the district of Matanzas, which offered so many opportunities for increasing one's fortune . . ."

Easing of the centuries-old prohibition against foreign commerce is correctly credited with the major responsibility for bringing prosperity to Cuba. At the same time, however, trade balances could not have continued to swell year after year, if the island's productive capacity had not been able to keep pace with the increased demand for Cuban produce from overseas markets. This latter problem was largely solved by the creoles themselves, who relied upon their own efforts rather than on the occasional favors which the Spanish Government might see fit to bestow.

Foremost among the native-born leaders stood Francisco de Arango y Parreño. His *Discourse on the Agriculture of Havana and Ways to Improve It,* which he sent to the Supreme Council of State early in 1792 for eventual inspection by King Charles IV, not only had a very great influence upon his contemporaries, but has been considered a classic of its kind ever since.

. . .

Before Arango's recommendations reached Madrid, the Crown had already extended for another six years a temporary decree which had previously opened the Cuban slave trade to all nations. Subsequent extensions followed in 1798 and 1804. Behind these events lay an essential point: that ". . . the trading element of Havana represented by Arango [had] joined forces with the liberalized government at home and secured practically free trade in slaves." That the officials governing Cuba during this period felt considerable concern for the island's economic welfare has already been shown elsewhere.

Some very human reasons at least partially account for this solicitude. Leading creole planters, to cite one case, had succeeded in drawing the Intendent, Valiente, into the sugar business. Captain-General Las Casas became an hacendado, when he acquired an ingenio in the Güines region and made considerable improvements on his new estate . . .

A near tidal wave of Africans seemed to inundate Cuba under official encouragement. Customs records reveal that over one quarter of a million Negroes passed through Havana between 1792 and 1821, while an additional sixty thousand reached the island through other authorized ports, like Santiago, or by the smuggler's time-honored channels . . .

Although Great Britain compelled the reluctant Spanish monarchy to accept a treaty abolishing the slave trade within its dominions in 1817 (to be effective in 1820), illicit importations continued the africanization of Cuba for many years. One careful analysis places the influx between the administrations of Captains-General Vives (1823–1831) and Dulce (1863–1865) at over three hundred thousand Negroes. This, it should not be forgotten, was in spite of increasingly strenuous efforts to suppress the traffic by British, French, and American naval patrols.

. . .

Africa had become an El Dorado for the mercantile class of Cuba, providing them with the surplus funds by which they held the planters in bondage. Guerra summarizes this interesting development as follows: ". . . the slave trade, which until the end of the eighteenth century had generally been a monopoly conceded by the Kings of Spain to foreign dealers, had passed into the hands of the richest merchants of Havana, whom it furnished with immense profits." An Italian traveler puts it more bluntly: "All large fortunes existing in Havana were made by trading in human flesh." But judged by their own ethical standards, persons who engaged in the slave trade, far from committing any crime against society, were making an essential contribution to the economic expansion of Cuba. . . .

Complaints against the slave trade in this era did not center about moral considerations. Rather, they manifested themselves in criticisms that it was unfair to give valuable concessions to certain favored individuals; that all Spanish subjects should compete under equal conditions. The Crown did not prove blind to steadily rising revenues from Cuba and granted all Spaniards another twelve years to import male Negroes (six years to foreigners) by a Royal Order of April 22, 1804. When Liberals in Spain began to speak of putting an end to the slave trade, it was not surprising that they stirred up a hornet's nest in Cuba. Through the *Real Consulado,* the *Sociedad Patriótica,* and the City Council of Havana, leading citizens (including Arango) addressed long and heated protests to the Spanish *Cortes* against such a dangerous course. There were probably very few whites on the island at that time who did not believe that abolition of the African trade would sound the death knell of Cuba's flourishing sugar and coffee industries.

Considering the tremendous profits realized, it was small wonder that the merchants of Havana jealously guarded their rights to virtually unlimited importation of Negro slaves, or that they began investing directly in expeditions to Africa. Returns on capital ventured ran well over one hundred percent. Therein lay perhaps the primary reason why planters could only borrow money at ruinous rates of interest. As Humboldt noted:

> The great profits made in the African slave trade, sometimes amounting to 100 or 125 percent, have contributed to increase the rate of interest; for many parties hire money at 18 or 20 percent, for the purpose of following this infamous trade.

. . .

Cuba's dramatic emergence as one of the world's richest countries dominates any review of the foregoing period. In the half century intervening between the reigns of Carlos III (1759–1788) and Isabel II (1833–1868), the number of sugar estates more than doubled. But during the same period exports of the sweet article multiplied seven-fold, indicating a tremendous increase of productive capacity among the island's sugar mills. This transformation, as we have seen, was largely owing to the skill with which some enlightened Spanish officials and various creole leaders were able to fish in the troubled waters of that storm-ridden era. Their ability to coöperate in capitalizing upon the devastation of St. Domingue, and the gradual decline of Jamaica, virtually assured Cuban domination of the world's cane sugar market.

These notable successes brought other results which proved hardly less significant for the future of Cuba. The rapid conversion from a pastoral Caribbean backwater into the world's sugar bowl produced an important class of *novi homines,* along with all of the excesses which usually mark the sudden rise of similar groups in every land. . . .

. . .

Inevitably, such a sudden accumulation of riches in the hands of a relatively few privileged families had its unwholesome side effects. One of Cuba's foremost scholars sums the situation up as follows:

> . . . a parasitic class developed upon slavery, an aristocracy of money derived through the exploitation of the African slave, which remained composed of natives, or Spaniards established in Cuba, and who troubled little, or not at all, about the care of their properties or of their business, these [being] under the care of administrators, stewards, and overseers whose management was liberally paid for. . . . Finally, the circumstance that [this] aristocracy of wealth might vacillate in its preference between Spain and the United States and vice versa, during a century, to maintain its privileges, would make it dependent upon the continuation of the colonial status in which Cuba had lived [so long already] . . . Every attempt designed to create and develop a Cuban economy, primarily geared to meet the basic needs of the [native] population with produce of the country, always encountered the opposition of that privileged class, which preferred to

make Cuba a nation exporting valuable staple crops and importing everything else.[2]

Further changes had been taking place in Cuban society as the result of immigration from former Spanish colonies on the American mainland. Like the Loyalists who settled in Canada or went back to Britain during the American Revolution, most of these arrivals had come to Cuba, rather than swear allegiance to a foreign flag. Often they had been roughly handled and lost all or most of their property. Understandably, then, they were usually more ardent in their support of royal authority than the newly landed peninsular Spaniards themselves. Oliver Cromwell's decision to implement "The Western Design" brought about the first important addition, when Penn and Venables seized Jamaica as a consolation prize for their failure to capture Hispañola. Possibly as many as fifteen hundred Jamaican colonists fled to Cuba, thereby increasing the island's sparse population by about ten percent.

By the Treaty of Paris, a century later, England returned Havana and Manila to defeated Spain, but demanded the Floridas as compensation. Consequently, a large portion of the white population in Florida followed the previous example of the Jamaicans and cleared out for nearby Cuba. Among his other concessions at the Peace of Basle, Godoy gave away the Spanish part of Española to the new French Republic, and this led to further departures for Cuba. When Toussaint l'Ouverture gained control of the whole island a few years later, thousands of Spanish colonists joined the stream of French refugees already seeking asylum in Cuba.

The return of Louisiana to France and its subsequent sale to the United States, in 1803, persuaded many disillusioned Spaniards—and with them not a few embit-

---

[2] Herminio Portell Vilá, *Historia de Cuba en sus Relaciones con los Estados Unidos y España,* I (Havana, 1938), 120.

tered French creoles—that it would be safer in the long run to start life all over again on the island of Cuba. Later on, cession of Florida to the United States drove most of the remaining Spanish inhabitants from that popular pawn on the international chessboard.

Finally, the successful revolt of the Spanish colonies from Tierra del Fuego to California unleashed yet another wave of immigration to Cuba. Droves of diehard Loyalists began flocking into Havana. After some three centuries of relative obscurity, the Great Antille now shone brightest among those few gems which still remained in the once dazzling Crown of Castile. . . .

. . .

On the other hand, it would be difficult to assert that this influx of colonial royalists turned out to be an unmixed blessing. Against the credit entries in Cuba's economic ledger, it is necessary to post some serious debits from a political standpoint.

> The concentration in Cuba of these Spanish Loyalists had naturally a positive influence on subsequent political developments and contributed to the success of the reaction which finally, in Cuba as well as in Spain, followed the Bourbon restoration after Napoleon's fall.

A situation of this nature scarcely augured well for the internal stability of Cuba in the years ahead. . . .

Tensions had always existed in Cuba between the creole and the native-born Spaniard, not that this represented any startling departure from colonial relationships elsewhere in the world. But continuing arrivals of aggressive royalists, from various quarters of the fast-disintegrating Spanish Empire in America, could only serve to exacerbate basic differences. More often than not, this type of immigrant made the peninsular Spaniard himelf seem moderate in his views by contrast. . . .

With few exceptions, then, it can probably be said that in general:

> The wealthy class of creoles was formed by the proprietors of sugar and coffee estates and of large stock farms. It depended upon the peninsular merchants for sale of agricultural products, acquisition of slaves and advancements of capital necessary to cover the overall costs of production. The interests of planters and merchants, given the monopolistic character of Spanish commerce and the financial domination which it exercised over agriculture were contradictory. . . . While the opposition between merchant and planter tended to increase, in as much as the first was [usually] a peninsular [Spaniard] and the second a creole, it took on a political aspect.[3]

Civil war still remained one generation in the future for Cuba, however; and the vested interests, creole or otherwise, usually lined up with the Crown. Faced with the choice between economic ruin or subservience to Spanish rule, most planters chose to remain on the side of law and order, no matter how odious this choice was to them personally. Perhaps it would be safer to say, apropos of this dilemma, that in actual practice the average hacendado usually tried to hedge his bets—to placate whichever side happened to be in control of his district at the moment, whether Spanish or Insurgent. But when Ferdinand VII died in 1833, civil war was not even a distant cloud on the horizon. More important, the island of Cuba had never been more prosperous.

---

[3] Ramiro Guerra y Sánchez, *Manual de Historia de Cuba* (Havana, 1938), p. 226.

20

FERNANDO ORTIZ

❁

Tobacco and Sugar: The Blending Which Produced the Culture of Cuba

---

Since 1906, Fernando Ortiz has been writing about different aspects of his country's culture. He has worked in such fields as linguistics, law, ethnography, and archaeology, and is the leading authority on Afro-Cuban culture. The book from which the following selection is taken provides a good example of this breadth of knowledge, combining as it does sociology, economics, and cultural history. The result is a colorful and profound interpretation of the development of Cuban society, a counterpoint produced by the dramatic dialogue between "Don Tobacco and Doña Sugar." Thus, modern Cuba was described by Ortiz in these symbolic terms:

From Fernando Ortiz, *Cuban Counterpoint: Tobacco and Sugar*, trans. Harriet de Onís (New York, Alfred A. Knopf, Inc., 1947), pp. 5–7, 51, 55–57, 65–66, 70–71. Reprinted by permission of the publisher.

> The marriage of tobacco and sugar, and the birth of alcohol, conceived of the Unholy Ghost, the devil, who is the father of tobacco, in the sweet womb of wanton sugar. The Cuban Trinity, tobacco, sugar, and alcohol.

The outstanding feature of our economic history is in reality this multiform and persistent contrast between the two products that have been and are the most typical of Cuba, aside from that period of brief duration at the beginning of the sixteenth century when the conquistadors' gold-mining activities and the cultivation of yucca fields and stock-raising to supply cassava bread and dried meat for the conquerors' expeditions took preëminence. Thus a study of the history of Cuba, both internal and external, is fundamentally a study of the history of sugar and tobacco as the essential bases of its economy.

And even in the universal history of economic phenomena and their social repercussions, there are few lessons more instructive than that of sugar and tobacco in Cuba. By reason of the clarity with which through them the social effects of economic causes can be seen, and because few other nations besides ours have presented this amazing concatenation of historical vicissitudes and this radical contrast, this unbroken parallelism between two co-existing orders of economic phenomena, which throughout their entire development display highly antithetical characteristics and effects, it is as though some supernatural teacher had purposely selected Cuba as a geographic laboratory in which to give the clearest demonstrations of the supreme importance of the basic economy of a nation in its continuous process of development.

. . .

In the economy of Cuba there are also striking contrasts in the cultivation, the processing, and the human connotations of the two products. Tobacco requires delicate care; sugar can look after itself. The one requires continual attention; the other involves seasonal work. Intensive versus extensive cultivation; steady work on the part of a few, intermittent jobs for many; the immigration of whites on the one hand, the slave trade on the other; liberty and slavery; skilled and unskilled labor; hands versus arms; men versus machines; delicacy versus brute force. The cultivation of tobacco gave rise to the small holding; that of sugar brought about the great land grants. In their industrial aspects tobacco belongs to the city, sugar to the country. Commercially the whole world is the market for our tobacco, while our sugar has only a single market. Centripetence and centrifugence. The native versus the foreigner. National sovereignty as against colonial status. The proud cigar band as against the lowly sack.

. . .

The machine won a complete victory in the sugar-manufacturing process. Hand labor has almost completely disappeared. The mechanization has been so thorough that it has brought about a transformation in the industrial, territorial, judicial, political, and social structure of the sugar economy of Cuba through an interlinked chain of phenomena which have not been fully appreciated by Cuban sociologists.

In the twentieth century the sugar production of Cuba reached the peak of its historical process of industrialization, even though it has not yet passed through all the phases necessary for its perfect evolutionary integration. Mechanization, which reached Cuba in the nineteenth century with the steam engine, began to triumph in that century and created the central; but it is in this twentieth century that the machine has given rise to the typical present-day organization, the super-central. This type of mill has been the logical outgrowth of mechanization, and from it have streamed a whole series of derivations that, because of their complicated interlocking structure and the relation of cause and effect, have not been clearly understood or properly analyzed. It is sufficient to point out here that the principal characteristics typical of the Cuban sugar industry today—and the same holds true in a greater or lesser degree of the other islands of the Antilles, and happens to a certain extent in other similar industries—are the following: mechanization, latifundism, sharecropping, wage-fixing, super-capitalism, absentee landlordism, foreign ownership, corporate control and imperialism.

. . .

The social consequences deriving from tobacco and sugar in Cuba and originating in the different conditions under which the two crops are produced can be easily grasped. The contrast between the vegas where tobacco is grown and the sugar plantation, particularly if it is a modern central, is striking. Tobacco gave origin to a special type of agricultural life. There is not the great human agglomeration in the tobacco region that is to be found around the sugar plants. This is due to the fact that tobacco requires no machinery; it needs no mills, nor elaborate physical and chemical equipment, nor railway transport systems. The vega is a geographical term; the central is a term of mechanics.

In the production of tobacco, intelligence is the prime factor; we have already observed that tobacco is liberal, not to say revolutionary. In the production of sugar it is a question of power; sugar is conservative, if not reactionary.

I repeat, the production of sugar was always a capitalistic venture because of its great territorial and industrial scope and the size of its long-term investments. Tobacco, child of the savage Indian and the virgin earth, is a free being, owing its neck to no mechanical yoke, unlike sugar, which is ground to bits by the mill. This has occasioned profound economic and social consequences.

In the first place, tobacco was raised on the land best suited for the purpose, without being bound to a great, indispensable industrial plant that was stationary and remained "planted" even after it had impoverished all the land about it. This gave rise to the central, which even in olden times was at least a village, and today a city. The vega was never anything but a rural holding, like a garden. The vega was small; it was never the site of latifundia, but belonged to small property owners. The central required a plantation; in the vega a small farm was enough. The owners of a central are known as hacendados and live in the city; those of the vegas remained *monteros, sitieros,* or *guajiros* and never left their rural homes.

The cultivation of tobacco demands a yearly cycle of steady work by persons who are skilled and specialized in this activity. Tobacco is often smoked to kill time, but in the tobacco industry there is no such thing as "dead time," as is the case with sugar. This, together with the circumstance that the vega was a small holding, has developed in the *veguero* a strong attachment to his land, as in the rancher of old, and made it possible for him to carry on his tasks with the help of members of his family. Only when this is not feasible does he hire workers, but in small groups, never gangs or by the hundred, as happens with sugar cane. The vega, I repeat, is merely a topographical denomination; the *colonia* is a term having complex political and social connotations.

. . .

The personal element always predominated in tobacco-growing, and there was a patriarchal, intimate equality about its work. Sugar was an anonymous industry, the mass labor of slaves or gangs of hired workmen, under the supervision of capital's overseers. Tobacco has created a middle class, a free bourgeoisie; sugar has created two extremes, slaves and masters, the proletariat and the rich. "There is no middle class in Havana, only masters and slaves," the Countess of Merlin wrote about her own country a century ago. Then she goes on to say: "The guajiro prefers to live on little for the sake of having his freedom." On the sugar plantations there existed the overlordship and the serfdom of underling and master; on the vegas there was the free industry of the humble peasant. The old colonial aristocracy of Cuba was almost always made up of rich planters on whom a title had been conferred because of their wealth in mills and slaves. Sugar titles rested on black foundations. The sprightly archpriest long ago observed:

> Suppose a man's an utter fool, a farmer or a boor,
> With money he becomes a sage, a knight with prestige sure;
> In fact, the greater grows his wealth the greater his allure,
> While he not even owns himself who is in money poor.

It is easy to see how the social organization involved in sugar production (mill and plantation) had, in addition to its capitalistic character, certain feudal and baronial features. Another clergyman, Juan de Castellanos, who was also a poet, put it very well in one of the thousands of verses that make up his famous *elegías:* "A plantation is a great estate." But he also said, referring to the plantations: "Each of these is a domain."

. . .

Tobacco has always been under the control of home government, economically and politically; whatever party has been in power in Cuba has been in control, for better or for worse, of tobacco. Sugar on the contrary, has been under foreign control superimposed on the island's government. The history of Cuba, from the days of the conquest to the present moment, has been essentially dominated by foreign controls over sugar, and the greater the value of our production, the greater the domination. During the centuries of the colonial period this power which was and is the controlling force in the economy of the Antilles was not, properly speaking, located in Madrid, inasmuch as ever since the sixteenth century the Spanish crown was only the legal machinery that, in exchange for the comfortable, well-paid, parasitical upkeep of its dynastic, aristocratic, military, clerical, and administrative bureaucracies maintained order among the peoples of the Peninsula and America and exploited their inhabitants under systems of feudalism and absolutism, leaving the economic initiative and control in the hands of the commercial, industrial, the financial capitalism of the more astute centers of Europe—Genoa, Augsburg, Flanders, London, and, in the nineteenth century, New York. By the same token we sons of free Cuba have sometimes asked ourselves whether our officials and politicians are serving the interests of our people or those of some anonymous sugar corporation, playing the part of deputized guards of the great Cuban sugar mill at the orders of foreign owners.

It is apparent from the foregoing that since the beginning of the sugar industry in the sixteenth century the whole history of Cuba has developed around this foreign domination which has always placed its own interests above those of the country. For this reason Cuban tobacco has had to bear the weight of export taxes levied against it for the benefit of the island's exchequer, whereas foreign-controlled sugar has always successfully evaded, until the present moment, which is exceptional, the payment of export duties to the Cuban Treasury Department even in those times, which today seem fabulous, when the returns on the capital invested in land, mill, and plantations was better than one hundred per cent. In the history of Cuba sugar represents Spanish absolutism; tobacco, the native liberators. Tobacco was more strongly on the side of national independence. Sugar has always stood for foreign intervention. But today, unfortunately, this capitalism, which is not Cuban by birth or by inclination, is reducing everything to the same common denominator.

21

SIDNEY W. MINTZ

The Industrialization of Sugar Production and Its Relationship to Social and Economic Change

---

In this introduction to the English translation of Ramiro Guerra y Sánchez' classic work on the sugar industry, Sidney W. Mintz presents a summary of the major themes of the Guerra book. In addition, he includes analyses of the impact of industrial technology on an agricultural society derived from his own work on the subject. Professor Mintz is a social anthropologist who has done extensive research on agricultural labor in the Caribbean. He is currently on the faculty of Yale University.

From Sidney W. Mintz, Foreword to Ramiro Guerra y Sánchez, *Sugar and Society in the Caribbean* (New Haven, Yale University Press, 1964), pp. xxii–xxvii, xxviii–xxix, xxxvii–xli. Reprinted by permission of the publisher.

In Cuba the renewed period of plantation growth began in the middle of the eighteenth century. Later, the Haitian revolution, wiping out as it did the richest sugar-producing colony of all, stimulated the growth of the plantation system in Cuba and Puerto Rico (though not in Spanish Hispaniola itself), and launched them on the path taken by their Dutch, English, French, and other predecessors.

Yet there were important differences, especially in the case of Cuba. By the time the plantation system began to expand in Cuba, that colony had a society, a people, and a culture of its own. We have seen that, for over two centuries, Cuba was able to build its society slowly, without protracted disturbance from the outside, and to avoid the plantation mode of development. One can justly refer to the growth of a "creole adaptation" in the Cuban setting. The economy rested heavily on small-scale agriculture (some of the products of which, such as tobacco and coffee, were processed and exported) and on livestock-raising (which provided food as well as export items such as hides and tallow).

The appearance and success of large numbers of substantially self-sufficient cultivators and small-scale peasant producers over the centuries was almost unique in the Caribbean; the other Hispanic colonies in the Antilles, Santo Domingo (till 1844) and Puerto Rico, most resembled Cuba in this regard. Though there were periods of isolation, and attempted invasions by other powers (Britain, for instance, occupied Havana for some months in 1763–64), Cuban society gradually took on a special quality: rural in emphasis, anti-Spanish but pro-Hispanic, folk-Catholic, creole. As the country developed a distinctive literature, music, dialect of Spanish, and national ideology, it acquired cultural integrity and solidarity as well.

Also contributing to the development of a distinctively Cuban society was the fact that, from the start of the sixteenth century until the middle of the eighteenth, the slave population of the island was provided with ample opportunities to become free. Spanish law, Catholicism, the slow rate of economic growth, and Iberian racial attitudes conspired to help the freedmen to integrate themselves in Cuban life swiftly and thoroughly. The percentage of Cuba's population which was of slave status was low at any point in the island's history, but it was particularly low before the 1760's. The contrast with the Antillean colonies of Britain, France, and The Netherlands was striking. Cuba was predominantly European in culture, but creolized; its population, both white and colored, lived mainly by independent farming and grazing, and its slaves were few. The colonies of other powers were, for the most part, populated by masses of slaves without any hope of improving their condition, and the only Europeans who inhabited these plantation settlements were overseers, government officials, and adventurers.

Cuba's near-uniqueness rested in her cultural synthesis, in the economic independence of her people, and in the protection she was provided against the spread of the plantation system. But the price of this protection and isolation was subjection to the imperial arbitrariness of the metropolis. It was Cuba's subsequent struggle in the 1860's and 1870's, for political and cultural autonomy from Spain which gave her the focus she needed to become a cohesive nation. Cuba as a Spanish colony had more nationhood than the colonies of the other European powers in the Antilles might have had as sovereign states.

It is because of this cultural integrity that Dr. Guerra, in his description of the spread of the plantation system in Cuba from the closing decades of the eighteenth century onward, assumes what some might regard as an unusually benign and undisturbed view of what happened. The fact is that the onrush of the plantation cycle made important changes in Cuban life, many of them malevolent. The intensification of slavery and the slave trade damaged civil liberties and increased the legal and social persecution of the slaves. The deterioration of civil liberties in Cuba was accompanied by an improvement in the economic situation of the country as a whole. Sugar and slavery might have boded ill for the rural poor; but they meant prosperity and expanded opportunity for the large-scale landowners. Somewhat ironically, Cuba's intensified plantation orientation developed precisely as the British and French West Indian colonies were disengaging themselves from this orientation. One famous student of colonialism could write, in the early nineteenth century, that the Spanish Antilles had been commonwealths when the British Antilles were factories; now, he continued, the Spanish islands were becoming factories, while he hoped that the British islands would soon be commonwealths.[1]

Cuba's push toward sovereignty was complicated by plantation prosperity and by the revival of the slavery issue. Spain had agreed (under British pressure) to outlaw the trade, but slaves continued to pour into Puerto Rico and Cuba. Slavery was not terminated until 1873 (or 1876, to mark the end of apprenticeship) in Puerto Rico, and until 1880 (1886) in Cuba; and slaves were transported illegally to these islands almost up to the moment of Emancipation. The last half-century of the trade—legally terminated by treaty in 1820, but continuing for about fifty years thereafter—probably added at least 200,000 slaves to the island population. So immense an increase (the population in 1877 was slightly more than a million and a half), even in a society with as much identity and shape as Cuba's, inevitably produced strains in the social system. One of Cuba's great historians, José Antonio Saco, was concerned with the "blackening" of Cuba's population. In fact, the physical type of the newcomers was irrelevant, except for what

[1] H. Merivale, *Lectures on Colonization and Colonies* (London: Longman, 1841), p. 39.

people might make of the difference. What mattered were the cultural differences and most of all, the differences in status, between free, native-born Cubans and the masses of enslaved, illiterate, newly arrived, and unacculturated migrants.

The apogee and gradual decline of the slave plantation era were marked not only by the smuggling-in of African slaves but also by the labor-contract importation of many thousands of Yucatecans and Chinese. These semi-free laborers eased the transition from slavery to freedom for the plantation owners by lowering the market price of free labor; thereby they took the burden of the transition upon their own backs. And at the same time that they added to the heterogeneity of Cuban society, they sorely taxed its existing social institutions. As with the slaves, it was not the physical type of the newcomers but their illiteracy, defenselessness against exploitation, cultural separateness, and degraded social status which made their integration difficult.

But Dr. Guerra may be right in feeling that none of these developments fundamentally altered the character of Cuban society. In the case of the English and the French Antilles, the slave plantation era had utterly erased the European yeoman colonist communities, supplanting these with great masses of African slaves under the control of a few Europeans. In such circumstances, it was almost impossible to create within the islands any cultural continuity, any informed social structure with potentialities for growth and development. Cuba, on the other hand, thanks to the late development of the slave plantation, had had time to create a society with character of its own.

As has been indicated, the slave plantations of the late eighteenth and early nineteenth centuries were larger and more advanced technically than those which preceded them, but they were not immense enterprises. Though operated with slave (and, later, contract) labor, the resident labor force was able to grow much of its food and to fabricate most of its basic domestic requirements. These plantations frequently had resident owners—Frenchmen or Spaniards, but mostly Cubans—and the relationships between the owners (*hacendados*) and the labor force were personal, if not congenial. The hacendados, usually rich and powerful men but not alien to the setting in which they functioned, were the community leaders. They and the men who worked for them as laborers or as slaves, as well as the small-scale cultivators of the countryside, were sometimes aligned politically against Spain and often in agreement on issues dealing with Cuban culture. That is, though the newly developing slave plantations powerfully affected Cuban society, it may be correct to assert that they were unable to change its basic character.

Thus, for instance, much Cuban land remained in subsistence crops and in tobacco, even at the height of slave-plantation expansion. Tobacco, an ideal small-farm crop requiring great personal care and skill to grow properly, was uniquely Cuban; its continuing importance and the contrast it made with sugar—so beautifully analyzed by Dr. Fernando Ortiz in *Cuban Counterpoint*—made clear that the slave plantation had not succeeded in entirely dominating Cuban rural life and values. Cuban novelists, poets, composers, and artists continued to contribute to the mainstream of New World life and letters. The National University remained an important center of learning. The bitter, seemingly endless struggle against Spain, which cruelly lay waste to Cuban lives and land, went on, giving meaning and poignance to *Cubanidad*—"Cuban-ness."

. . .

In Dr. Guerra's view, the political, social, and economic changes which overtook Cuba after 1898 were more penetrating and powerful than anything which had come before. These changes cannot be divorced from United States interests in the Caribbean area. It is important to remember that the technical revolution had come before the United States occupation. In the two decades immediately preceding the occupation, the sugar industry had shaken itself down, so to speak. Small enterprises were replaced by large ones; small mills were eliminated and their surrounding lands preëmpted by large mills. Integrated productive assemblages of mills and land became larger, and the small-scale community nature of the traditional plantations was undermined by the change in scale and in mode of operation. But it was only under the aegis of North American power that the earlier changes were extended throughout the sugar industry and the whole industry vastly enlarged.

. . .

Dr. Guerra points out that the plantation (or latifundium) is an urbanizing force. As such it urbanizes while it proletarianizes. By creating company towns, by appropriating large areas within which the rural population must concentrate itself densely, by bringing improvements in transportation and communication, by standardizing work practices, by establishing company stores, the latifundium does its powerful best to create a factory situation, albeit a rural one. And factories in the field are urban in many ways, even though they are not in cities. A rural proletariat working on modern plantations inevitably becomes culturally and behaviorally distinct from the peasantry. Its members neither have nor (eventually) want land. Their special economic and social circumstances lead them in another direction. They prefer standardized wage minimums, maximum work weeks, adequate medical and educational services, increased buying power, and similar benefits and protections. In these ways, they differ both from the peasantry—who are often conservative, suspicious, frugal, traditionalistic—and from the farmers, who are the agricultural businessmen, the forward-looking, cash-oriented, rural middle class. Such differentiations do not exhaust the sociology of the Cuban countryside; but at least they indicate that to talk of Cuba's "peasantry" as if the rural population were an undifferentiated mass of impoverished landowners is to miss entirely the complexity of rural Latin America. Peasants who, by a swift process of plantation development, have been transformed into rural proletarians, are no longer the same people.

It was the latifundium which converted Cuba's socially heterogeneous rural areas into plantation complexes. Dr. Guerra shows us how this conversion displaced the independent farmers, weakened the rural middle classes (even while bringing more cash income into the countryside), eliminated subsistence cultivation, created total dependence on cash for its landless employees, and stimulated political consciousness on a class basis. The landless, wage-earning, store-buying, organized countrymen—*not* peasants—who had nothing to sell but their labor (and that little more than five months a year) were perfectly ripened by *latifundismo* for changing their economic perceptions into political action.

When it is noted that, in 1953, there were 489,000 agricultural wage laborers in Cuba and 67,000 unpaid family laborers, a gross indication of the difference between peasantry and proletariat is provided us. Many of the agricultural wage laborers did not work for plantations; but many and probably most of the unpaid family laborers were the wives and children of the traditional, small-scale highland peasantry—*los guajiros*—of Cuba. More than 21 out of every 100 members of the *total* labor force worked in the agricultural phases of sugar production alone and in harvest time the percentage rose; more than 60 out of 100 worked for wages. These data reveal the enormous extent to which Cuba was precisely *not* a peasant country; in fact it was because the peasantry was losing ground to the encroaching latifundium that Dr. Guerra could become so justly concerned for the fate of his country.

But the figures are yet more revealing when combined with those for landownership and control. The 1946 Census indicated that 20 percent of the farmed area was held by less than one tenth of one percent of the farms—that is, one fifth of all Cuban farmland was divided up among slightly more than one hundred farms. Of the total number of farms, 70 percent were 63 acres or less in area, but accounted for only 11 percent of the farmland. In other words, the Cuban land situation was archetypal for Latin America: a bimodal distribution, with a few enormous latifundia at one end and many very small farms at the other.

But the dichotomy in Cuba goes farther than this, since the large units were mainly sugar plantations—modern, heavily capitalized, and powerful—and where they spread, the small independent farm disappeared. By and large, the difference between peasantry and proletariat was the difference between highland and plain, between small and large, between other crops and sugar cane, and—some would argue—between white and black. Sugar is a lowland crop, a plantation crop, a colonial crop. Before emancipation as well as after, Cuban plantation owners felt the pinch of labor shortage and filled their needs with outsiders.

The special significance of this process—literally, of converting a nation where land could still be secured by landless free men into one in which this would not be feasible—is not missed by Dr. Guerra. Labor shortage is a relative matter. The importations of African slaves and, later, of contract laborers from Mexico and China were political acts with economic objectives: to secure labor at a lower price and to make it more tractable. After the turn of the century, neither slavery nor contract importations from China and India were possible. The plantation owners turned instead to the other Antilles, to the descendants of the slaves in Haiti and

Jamaica. These migrants came to Cuba because the expanding plantations there gave them greater economic opportunities than they had at home. But of course they won these expanded economic opportunities at the cost of the landless Cuban rural poor who had come before them, and the Cuban people were well aware of it. Between 1912 and 1924, 120,000 Haitians and 110,000 Jamaicans came as contract laborers to Cuba. Their effect on labor conditions in Cuba can be readily imagined.

The North American dream, that sons may fulfill fathers' ambitions, was rarely realized by the children of the Chinese, Jamaican, or Haitian migrants to Cuba. Their descendants could not be certain that their integration into Cuban life would be either rapid or successful. The latifundium system was directly responsible for the heightened importation of migrant workers into Cuba, as the earlier slave plantation system had been responsible for the importation of smuggled slaves and Chinese and Yucatecan contract laborers. These people were imported for the hardest and poorest-paying labor of all—cane-cutting—and could rarely find work outside harvest season if they stayed on. Unlike immigrants to North America, they could not readily become part of an expanding economy, since the sugar industry dominated that economy entirely; all they could do was to force further downward the levels of living of the Cuban people.

Thus, in the early decades of this century, Dr. Guerra suggests, Cuba was becoming a country in which the best land was owned on a large scale and by foreigners, and worked by foreigners as well. His words in this connection ring strangely:

> A country which is politically unfree, but which possesses and cultivates its own lands, can win its freedom, as Cuba did. But a free people who relinquish their land to another have taken the path to economic servitude and social and political de-

cay. . . . Within a quarter of a century, either the latifundium or the republic will no longer exist. The Cuban people will have land and independence, or they will have lost them both. That, not annexation, is Cuba's manifest destiny in the twentieth century.

22

WILLIAM APPLEMAN WILLIAMS

❋

The Influence of the United States on the Development of Modern Cuba

---

The influence of the United States on the economic and social development of twentieth-century Cuba has generally been accepted by scholars, but there is much controversy concerning the exact nature and the consequences of this influence. Professor William A. Williams believes that the policies and actions of the United States not only exerted a profound influence on the society and economy of Cuba, but also on its political and ideological development.

William A. Williams is a professor of history at the University of Wisconsin. His numerous books

---

From William A. Williams, "Cuba: Issues and Alternatives," *Annals of the American Academy of Political and Social Science,* CCCLI (January, 1964), pp. 73–78. Reprinted by permission of the American Academy of Political and Social Science.

and articles have challenged many standard interpretations in the areas of U.S. foreign policy and intellectual history. This essay stems from his concern with the relationship between U.S. foreign policy and revolutions.

The historic and traditional factors, which have been operating since 1895, involve American control and penetration in Cuba, the structural consequences of that power, and the ideas that evolved in the deployment and use of that authority. A consciousness of the power and a determination to use it in keeping with an American definition of Cuba became apparent as early as President Grover Cleveland's annual message of December, 1895. The United States sought the prompt and permanent pacification of the island under circumstances that would insure military control of the island and that would facilitate and safeguard United States' economic predominance.

President William McKinley ultimately initiated war to effect that kind of pacification. He did so with the blunt—if usually overlooked or forgotten—explanation that the United States thereby set itself in opposition to the Cuban revolutionaries as well as to the Spanish government. He chose not to recognize the Cubans because that would "subject us to embarrassing conditions of international obligation" toward them. He accepted the corollary that the United States would be involved in "hostile constraint" against the revolution as well as the Spanish overlords.

Cuba was first to be pacified, then to be reconstructed along lines satisfactory to the United States, and finally—and only finally—to be handed over to the Cubans after such vital limits on their freedom of action and development had been established. Like all imperial regulations, the American ground rules specified a relationship of superior to inferior. They imposed a direction upon, and set the allowable means for, the economic, political, and social development of Cuban society. The system was self-defeating: not only was Cuba denied access to any effective bargaining power vis-à-vis the United States but also the nature of the limits imposed made it impossible for Cuba to achieve either the goals set by American leaders or the objectives defined by its own traditions and aspirations.

. . .

One way of establishing the agreed-upon conditions involved making Cuba into a traditional kind of colony. But this solution was criticized as contradicting the idea, ideal, and experience of America's traditional expanding market place. It was also attacked on the grounds that the domestic costs—political and social as well as economic—of traditional empire were exorbitant. The instruments required to establish and maintain that kind of empire might easily destroy the very free-enterprise capitalism that it was supposed to guarantee.

The resolution of these problems came through two ideas. One of them, formulated as the Open Door policy, set the strategy of establishing the principle of an open field with no favors as the basis for competition with other imperial powers. Given such access to the world market place, Americans were confident that they could whip their rivals and thus create a new frontier over and over again in all the underdeveloped areas of the world. The second idea held that in cases like Cuba, where it was necessary to establish outposts of American power, the traditional colonial dilemma would be resolved by exercising only such controls as were necessary to mold the society along the essential lines of the United States. This would ease the moral crisis defined by expansion per se, develop the subject societies so that they could be integrated into the greater American market place, and do both of those things in a way that assured indefinite American predominance.

This combination of interests and ideas produced policies and actions that structured Cuban society within well-defined limits. American control restored and consolidated the free-labor, one-crop sugar economy with its chronic underemployment and unemployment, reinforced the traditional pattern of land and crop control, and tied the trade and service sectors of the Cuban economy to the American market. The result was an informal empire in which the urban-rural imbalance was sustained and even intensified.

The political consequences of this pattern involved the exclusion of the great majority of Cubans from any meaningful participation in formulating or choosing between alternatives for their own society. Cuban society became characterized by extremes of stratification and by a propensity to develop as two cultures. One of these, the numerically smaller, evolved as a Cuban-American society in which Cuban traditions, ideas, and ideals underwent continuing and skewed mutation in the direction of American culture. The history of Havana, for example, provides an excellent illustration of how this distortion and alienation occurred.

The second culture remained far more Cuban and Latin and far more lower class and agrarian. This lower-class, majority culture did not escape American influence. But the impact of the American images, symbols, and artifacts of material progress was in some respect counterbalanced by the anticolonial and potentially revolutionary tradition inherent in American history. This tradition was introduced by American leaders as a justification and defense of their empire in Cuba. Once in circulation, however, it served to some degree to reinforce the drive of the native Cuban culture to win independence and establish its own values.

Against this possibility, the United States explicitly reserved the right to intervene if the underlying and direct controls in the American system proved ineffective. Military action was authorized by the Platt Amendment, which also made it clear that the United States would block any Cuban effort to modify the system by using a third power as a fulcrum on which to rest the lever of Cuban nationalism, and thereby to pry the imperial system loose at its foundations. Such force was used by all categories of American leadership—Democratic and Republican, liberal and conservative.

This description and analysis of basic American policy has served also to outline the structure within which Cubans had to operate. Against that background, the long-range factors affecting and limiting Cuban development can be described under three broad headings.

Physical and cultural factors made it impossible for Cuba ever to meet the American criteria for freedom by achieving a fundamental likeness to the United States. This underlying axiom of American policy was impossible by history and economic geography as well as by definition. . . .

. . .

Cuba could move *toward* the specified goal of becoming a miniature America, and, in some respects, it did develop in that fashion and direction during the sixty-three years of American rule. But the analogy is not to progression through an arithmetic series to a finite number but, rather, to arithmetic progression toward infinity which renders each step far smaller than it may seem to those who take it—or those who want it taken. In reality, furthermore, there is a point beyond which success in such transformation creates an increasing opposition to further change of that kind.

American policy thus launched Cuban society on a voyage into a cul-de-sac. American economic predominance developed in such a manner, and in such a short period of time, for example, that it thwarted the rise of any sizable, indigenous, Cuban capitalist class. In practice as well as in definition, a capitalist must have the power and the freedom to develop and choose between significant entrepreneurial alternatives, and this range of choices must include the sources and terms of capital accumulation. To cite one illustration from American history, capitalists rely in certain phases of their development on a running national debt as a means of accumulating capital, yet this crucial device was denied to the Cubans by American leaders. Cuban capitalists lacked other similar freedoms because of the power of various Americans who made such decisions formally or informally.

Cubans thus became at best limited participants and more generally simply agents and instruments in an American empire. Even the most fortunate could not become entrepreneurs save within that system. Cubans might become property-owning middle-class businessmen, but their property did not give them any significant power in the system per se. Furthermore, American policy did not develop Cuba rapidly enough even to create sufficient openings to meet either the expectations or the needs of this group.

Upper-class Cubans also lacked the power traditionally associated with their position in a society. They were wealthy, they lived in a pseudoaristocratic manner, and they exercised considerable power and authority over other Cubans. But they could not and did not define the limits, establish the direction and momentum, or create a style for their society in the manner of a true ruling class. Given the island's natural wealth, it is not inconceivable that a Cuban upper class could adapt the traditional Latin and Catholic traditions of a corporate society to the conditions of the modern world. Indeed, the Cuban constitution of 1940 manifests the persistence of those traditions and is in part the result of an effort to construct a neocorporatist instrument of government. But even those conservative traditions, with their emphasis upon nationalism and upon the government's role in economic and social development, challenged the established pattern of American predominance.

As a result, Cuban conservatives had to fall back upon the strategy of establishing and maintaining a liaison with American economic and political leaders, official and unofficial. This limited what they *could* do and further slowed the rate and extent of economic and social development. Cuba was by 1955 approaching the limits that American policy and action imposed upon the island. Instead of opening possibilities, American policy limited opportunities and moved toward stagnation at what can be termed a high level of underdevelopment. And it is very doubtful whether even that degree of success would have been achieved without the subsidy provided by World War II and the Cold War.

American control operated to polarize Cuban politics and ideology. The system per se had to be changed before even reforms of a significant nature could be introduced. This meant that consequential politics became increasingly revolutionary, not only in terms of domestic affairs but also in terms of Cuba's relationship to the United States. American policy thus functioned to create an indigenous radical movement.

. . .

One kind of action might possibly have indefinitely delayed a Cuban revolution led by indigenous radicals. A basic modification in American policy designed to assist the Cuban upper class in generating inclusive economic and social development might have undercut the structural support for radical leadership. This would have been very difficult, however, even if American policymakers had made the necessary changes in their own outlook. For not only had the Cuban upper class increasingly abandoned its own traditional guidelines under the pressure for Americanization but the Cuban middle class had done likewise. By the mid-1950's, at any rate, Cuban upper-class leaders trying to adapt and act upon a corporate program would have met serious opposition from within their own class as well as from the middle class and from Cuban radicals.

23

LOWRY NELSON

The Social Class Structure

Writing in 1950, Professor Lowry Nelson stated: "In a strictly economic and political sense one might be justified in postulating a middle class in Cuba, but in the more subtle, psychological sense it is very doubtful that the classification would be valid." This view has been attacked by some scholars. In the same Pan-American Union symposium which featured Nelson's view, Carlos Manuel Raggi Ageo propounded a thesis almost diametrically opposed. He concluded that a majority of Cubans were middle class in status.[1] This problem still needs much study, but the fact that such a controversy exists illustrates the dilemma of social identification which did face those Cubans who were neither rich nor poor. Nelson's emphasis on ideas and attitudes is quite important in this context, since a person's

---

From Lowry Nelson, "The Social Class Structure," *Materiales para el estudio de la clase media en la America Latina* (Washington, D.C., Pan American Union, 1950), II, 47–48, 50–55. Reprinted by permission of the publisher.

[1] Carlos Manuel Raggi Ageo, "Contribución al estudio de las clases medias en Cuba," *Materiales para el estudio de la clase media en la America Latina* (Washington, D.C., Pan American Union, 1950), II, 74–89.

belief concerning his social status and the social values which he accepts are vitally important elements in the decisions which he makes. Income statistics alone tell only part of the story about a nation's social class structure.

Lowry Nelson has been involved in rural sociology both as an academician and as a public official in state and national agencies. For a number of years he was a professor of sociology at the University of Minnesota.

It is a temptation for the observer of Cuban life to conclude that the class structure consists of an "upper" and a "lower" class, or even more likely, "upper," "middle," and "lower," and let the statement stand. But to do so would oversimplify greatly what in reality is a complex situation. This observer is not at all certain that a middle class exists, but there can be no doubt about the upper and lower classes. These appear to be well marked. Within these classes, however, there are complex variations; so complex, in fact, as to make generalization hazardous. One has the general feeling that Cuban society has not set or jelled. While the island has had a history of European contact which dates back a century before permanent white settlement in the United States, this contact has been complicated by various crosscurrents. Unlike most of the other Hispano-American cultures, that of Cuba is not a result of the mixture of the Spanish and indigenous cultures, but rather that of two exotic cultures, the Spanish and African, with only slight admixtures of French, Anglo-Saxon, and Chinese. Moreover, Cuban society has been in a state of political, economic, and social turbulence and instability for approximately a century.

Its political unrest did not end with the gaining of

independence after practically a half-century of struggle, but has continued during the period of the Republic, while the country was experiencing the birth pangs of bringing forth a national state. Its economic system, geared to the fortunes of its dominant crop, sugar, has suffered extreme fluctuations throughout its history, and has not yet reached a point of stability. These conditions have affected inevitably the entire social structure. A political or governing class has emerged; wealth has been accumulated by way of speculation and expansion in its basic industry. Extremes of wealth and poverty are juxtaposed.

In this matrix of events there has been considerable mobility up and down the social hierarchy. People who were rich have been made poor, some who were poor were made rich; some of them have become richer; and great masses of the poor have been pushed farther down the scale. Cuban society, as a stable and organized structure, can properly be regarded as in a state of emergence. It would hardly be true to say that the Cuban state is "an almost hypothetical entity" because there is no "Cuban society," as one native writer has said, for, where human beings live together as long as have the Cubans, there is a society, although its description may be difficult because its outlines are not clearly marked. Nevertheless, Miguel de Carrión expressed a feeling which any observer of Cuban life is likely to experience, a feeling of bafflement.

. . .

In the first place, it is clear that the Spanish inheritance is largely feudal in its nature. Feudalism recognized an upper class (nobles, both secular and ecclesiastical) possessed of rights of ownership of land and other forms of wealth; and a lower class, who although they possessed certain rights, generally did not have the right to own land. Moreover, the rights of the lower class were in general those granted by the upper. The duties were also apportioned. The duty of working the land, of doing the menial tasks, fell, of course, upon the lower class. The upper class had the duty of defending them against the depredations of competing nobles, and especially the duty of governing and dispensing justice. The upper class was not expected to do menial tasks, nor would they stoop to do them. They were waited upon by slaves and servants, who attended to all their personal wants. Significantly, also, women were especially distinct as between the two classes. Upper-class women had few responsibilities either for the care of their home or for the rearing of their children. These were the responsibilities of the servants and nurses. The age of chivalry placed women (that is upper-class women) on pedestals, and practically rendered them helpless for any purpose other than to be admired. They had little or no competence in the arts of homemaking and no opportunity to learn them.

. . .

The emancipation of women has been one important aspect of the social evolution of society during the nineteenth century. An important part of this movement has been the acceptance of ever larger responsibilities on the part of the women of the upper classes especially, notably those in what may be loosely called the "middle class." Women of such status in the United States, for example, do their own housework with a minimum of domestic help. They care for their own children, do their own marketing, and generally operate their own households.

In Cuba, the feudal acceptance of upper and lower class positions, rich and poor, is still a dominant feature of society. The criada speaks of "us poor people" and of "the rich people." The well-to-do Cuban would not allow his wife to do any housework, because that would lower her to the status of servant. The daughter is not allowed to soil her hands in the kitchen. She must be kept "lovely" for the husband who is to be. The children of white Cubans are cared for by a colored or lower-class white nurse. It is she who gets them ready for school, washes their clothes, takes them to the carrousel and supervises them throughout their waking hours.

The upper-class Cuban women of the cities, therefore, have little or no household responsibilities, except that of general supervision. Cooking, washing, scrubbing, and caring for the children are tasks performed by servants. While this relief from drudgery should free them for active and effective participation in public affairs, it is the exceptional woman who takes advantage of the opportunity thus afforded, or who feels justified in going against the ancient tradition that her place is in the home.

. . .

The upper-class Cuban husband assumes very few of the menial responsibilities which are almost universally accepted by his counterpart in the United States. For example, he would not expect to fix a leaky water-tap, or repair light switches, mow the lawn, look after the garden, and certainly not to wash his own automobile. These are the tasks for the *chofer* and the gardener and the poor boy who seeks to earn a few pennies for cleaning out the garage. They are tasks reserved for the lower class.

This difference between rich and poor is widely recognized in Cuba in other ways. One will see, for example, a school labelled *para niños pobres* (for poor children). During the Christmas season the First Lady of the Land distributes gifts to the "poor people" in front of the Presidential Palace. Thus the poor congregate ostentatiously before the palace in great numbers to receive their gifts. The point is not that gifts are given to the poor—an act that is done in most countries—but solely in the manner of public giving, which amounts to official recognition of a class called "the poor." While this may be regarded as commendable realism, as contrasted with the practice in the United States of protecting the sensibilities of the poor by taking the gift to the home, it would seem to fortify, by public recognition, the status of being poor.

24

JUAN BOSCH

❋

The National Psychology

Of all the ways of interpreting Cuba perhaps none is more fascinating—and more subjective—than the psychological. Impressionistic in methodology, subject to few tools of objective verification, and often simplistic in approach, this vehicle must be used with care. Yet, when employed by a knowledgeable observer who is in tune with the culture, insights are developed which sometimes elude the scientific student. Juan Bosch is such an observer. His interpretation of Cuban psychology helps to illuminate the life of the island, and adds flesh and blood to the more scholarly analyses.

Bosch is a poet, novelist, and sometime politician who struggled for years to bring reform to his native Dominican Republic. At present he is again in exile after having been ousted as president by the *golpe de estado* of September, 1963. He is living in Puerto Rico and lectures on public administration at the University of Puerto Rico.

Translated from Juan Bosch, *Cuba: La isla fascinante* (Santiago de Chile, Editorial Universitaria, S.A., 1955), pp. 169–175, 182–187.

The Cuban wants money in order to render homage to his wife. This is a historical theory I have come up with in order to explain to myself the traditional lack of honesty which exists in the country in the administration of public money. In Cuba, since the most remote colonial days, those with fiscal duties enrich themselves; and it is only recently that a national movement demanding clean administration has begun. And I have come up with my theory, half because of its humor and half because every day the opulent beauty of the Cuban woman amazes me. Hence when a stranger asked me why it happens that in public offices so much money is stolen from the people, I answered, pointing to the first girl who passed by: for that reason—because women so beautiful require, even though they don't ask for it, an environment of comfort and splendor. Her presence alone inclines man to offer her the finest and the most beautiful.

The superficial explanation was often well received, which suggests that perhaps there may be a little truth in it. Certainly, there must be other traits which would throw some light on that national evil. The very absence of inhibitions, for example. The Cuban doesn't have them; but because he doesn't have them, he has not been accustomed to imposing any limit upon himself. Everything that seems conventional to him bothers him.

There is the case of courtesy. In a natural way, without words, the Cuban pays attention to his friend. As he is generous, he doesn't let anyone pay where he is if he has money left; he offers his last good cigar as if he carried a dozen on him; he would be incapable of enjoying one hour of abundance and pleasure without anyone to share it with him. But he is not courteous—at least not in the conventional sense of the word. If he has to speak, he doesn't lower his voice, though it be the middle of the night and people are sleeping. He turns on the radio full blast; it does not matter whether his neighbor likes it or not. And it is very difficult for him to stop his automobile to let a pedestrian, or even the driver who follows him, go by. On the same level, the Cuban is not very practical. Why live in poverty if there is money?

The people, as such, are among the most honorable in the world. In Havana, in every respect a great city, there are hardly two or three robberies a day. The streets sleep overstocked with automobiles which no one watches, and unless there is an urgent need for tires or spare parts, as there was during World War II, in the morning they are exactly as their owners left them the night before. But with public money Cuban conduct is different. If there is plenty, the best thing is to take it. During two years of service, for instance, a minister appropriated about forty-eight million dollars and brought it to Miami; when he was asked how he had been able to take so much money out of Cuba, he answered with the greatest naturalness: "In suitcases."

There is no doubt that together with a history of riches which seems like the work of miracles, the lack of inhibitions of the Cuban inclines him to a kind of megalomania. There is nothing that a Cuban doesn't feel capable of doing. That minister who with such surprising simplicity explained how he had taken forty-eight million dollars was in a state of megalomania; and this condition often reaches unsuspected heights. Fulgencio Batista was a megalomaniac when at the head of sergeants and corporals, he raised in rebellion the army and navy in a country which counted hundreds of distinguished, trained officers; the Cubans who rose against Spain were oblivious of the possible consequences when they faced, without any arms other than some old rifles and liberator machetes, the veteran armies organized and composed of thousands of well-equipped troops. The admirable and often incomprehensible aspect of Cuba is that evil-seeming megalomania at times becomes a virtue.

. . .

Reading the Cuban press or listening to its radio, a stranger might at first believe that a national disgrace is imminent. One is overcome by the sense of general instability. It astonishes the stranger to see, at the end of a week, that the people still have not yet attacked the national treasury building, that the crowd hasn't sacked the presidential palace, that a horrendous crime hasn't taken place every twenty-four hours, that women can walk alone late at night on the avenues and streets without anyone molesting them.

The Cuban is not aware of that exciting climate which surrounds him. The Cuban lives a life of agitation, but only in appearance. His excitement—and this is one of the great mysteries of the national genius—seems to be a way of collecting all his inner energies in order to direct them single-mindedly toward the conquest of happiness by the jubilant route of hedonism. The Cuban has a talent for pleasure.

When I pronounce what I have just written, those who think in terms of philosophy and sociology open their eyes and look at me askance from the height of their knowledge. But I insist that the Cuban has a talent for hedonism. It requires a special blend of feeling and intelligence such as the Cubans have: the gift of understanding the juicy essence of pleasure in each thing or the correct shade called for to produce the full rapture of enjoyment. From his most tender infancy the Cuban knows how to distinguish between the beautiful and the ugly, and between the good and the bad when these values refer to qualities. An instinctive wisdom directs him toward the pleasant. He lives with his body and he tries not to wear it out. He enjoys dancing as if the music was passing in rapid ascent through his bones and his veins. He knows, almost by divination, good food, the better material, the best perfume. And he passes through the world psychologically comfortable, because he flees inhibitions and doesn't fear his complexes.

. . .

. . . The Cuban never cheats. He can lie; he can make a promise which later on he may not be able to keep. But as far as it refers to himself, how he is or isn't, he doesn't cheat. What angers him, angers him, be it moral or immoral; and he says so. Without delay or preamble, he exposes his purposes; and when he has to speak well of himself, he does it with as much spontaneity and as much fire as when he has to inform you of his weakness.

Sincerity is not a virtue in Cuba; it is a daily, simple, elementary fact. This explains why the Cuban needs public liberty, which he couldn't live without. To try to do violence to that people, to keep them from protesting, judging, or expressing their feeling is madness, because they are accustomed to protest about themselves, to judge themselves, to express without qualification what they think. The government which doesn't respect that manifestation of the national genius will be repudiated unanimously.

. . .

Relajo . . . is the result of a hatred of order; as *Choteo* is hatred for the solemn. Relajo is a man's liberty to act as he wishes. Some Cuban thinker or other who has not understood the national genius of his country has complained because Cuba has [not] been converted into a methodical country, ruled by logic, where the people arrive for their engagements on the dot, where the bureaucrats work until the last minute, where the politicians speak with impartiality. He doesn't know that Cuba was formed by people without any law but their will, accustomed to rebel against the threat of imminent death; and that afterwards the island was, with few intervals a center of continually increasing riches; and with that tradition and the easy living, the people who produced the riches did not submit to discipline . . . And finally, the upper classes gave no example to support their claim to conduct different from the masses.

. . .

Often the makers and guiders of public opinion, politicians and thinkers, undertake to give new sense to the life of a nation. But if they don't understand the national character of that nation, they mistake the road. Benito Mussolini erred by trying to make Italy—a land of artists, philosophers, and people who love life—into a nest of imperial eagles, bristling with machine guns and populated by the voices of bugles. Italian fascism lasted as long as the Italians didn't have to use their armies; then it was proven that Mussolini had built on false foundations because the national character of Italy didn't call it to wars of conquest. The national character of Cuba doesn't call the fascinating island to a life of order.

And we must thank the gods that it is this way. Since in a world where industrial order, manufacturing sternness, and the logic of machines keep the crowds under the threat of the next war when the echoes of the last one haven't yet died—and we have walked this path for many long decades—the free living of the Cubans is an enchanting backwater, a bewitching, moral bay where God's creatures find sustenance, feeding themselves on the happiness of living in order to carry the weighty burden of a humanity tiring out and filling up with bitterness.

The stranger who passes through Cuba winds up loving the relajo. He admits, of course, that the philosophers and politicians are trying to correct it and trying above all to constrict it until it is converted into a vice. The people themselves know, however, up to what limit they should use it, because one often hears on the lips of a woman, an old man, a learned scholar, or a worker, when a certain limit is reached: "El relajo con orden, gentlemen." What we would like understood about the Cuban's love of life, such as it is, without falsifying it or turning it into ridiculous theories, is that in that struggle against the enchanting relajo, one arrives at a point of examining its suitability and usefulness. Then, on the contrary the day will come in which we will hear other voices advise: "El orden con relajo, gentlemen."

25

DUDLEY SEERS

Economic and Social Problems of Twentieth Century Cuba

The most objective studies of the Castro Revolution have been written by Europeans and Latin Americans. The volume from which the following selection was taken is an excellent example of this. Two English and two Chilean economists collaborated in this study. In the introductory chapter Dudley Seers (the editor) provides a cogent analysis of the pre-1959 socio-economic problems of Cuba, with special emphasis on the related factors of fluctuation and instability.

Seers has had a three-fold career: as a teacher at Oxford and Yale, as government consultant, and as United Nations official. Currently he is director of the Division of Trade and Surveys of the U.N. Economic Commission for Africa.

From Dudley Seers, *et al., Cuba: The Economic and Social Revolution* (Chapel Hill, N.C., University of North Carolina Press, 1964), pp. 6–9, 11–13, 17–19. Reprinted by permission of the publisher.

Being a sugar economy was not always a burden for Cuba. After the successful revolution against Spain (1896–98), there was a very fast development of sugar for the United States market. During the first quarter of this century, sugar output and exports rose rapidly, with the help of American capital, and this rise led to general increases in activity in other sectors, such as transport, energy, and construction. It seems from the data available that in the years from 1912 to 1924, Cuban living conditions were not low by international standards then current—per-capita income in 1922–25 averaged over $200 in current prices, according to very tentative estimates; this would be at least $400 at the prices of the mid-1950's. From another point of view, this figure was more than 35 percent of per capita income in the United States, which was about $600 at that time.

But this upward climb showed signs of slackening even in the 1920's. There was a short but ominously severe break in the sugar market in 1920; after 1924 exports leveled off, with prices settling at 2 to 3 cents a pound. From 1929, prices and volumes both started to slide and sugar exports dropped to very low levels. . . . In 1933 and 1934, the dollar value of these exports was less than one quarter of what it had been a decade earlier. A recovery brought exports up to quite a high level again in the 1940's, but once more there was a lag in the 1950's, relieved only temporarily by sales of $656 million in 1957; in 1958 they had fallen back to $594 million.

Even the apparent rise between the 1920's and the 1940's in the value of exports was partly due to price rises. The physical output of sugar climbed from about 1 million tons a year in 1905 to 5 million in 1925, but a level of 5 to 6 million was typical of the years 1947 to 1958, apart from the quite exceptional crop of 7 million in 1952. There was, in consequence, no need to build any more sugar mills after 1925, and in fact the number of mills in operation declined from 184 in 1926 to 161 in 1958. . . .

Reasons for the poor performance of exports are not difficult to find. Cuban exports depended very much on what she sold to the United States, easily her best customer up to 1960. In turn, these sales depended on: 1. the income of the United States; 2. the relation between income and the demand for sugar; and 3. the allocation of U.S. consumption between various suppliers.

. . .

. . . The purchasing power of Cuban exports in 1952–56 was no more than it had been thirty years earlier, whereas in the period from 1902–06 to 1922–26 their purchasing power had more than doubled.

The stagnation in sugar affected the whole economic picture, for no other major sectors emerged to stimulate the economy. Other forms of agriculture expanded, but not very rapidly. Mineral output fluctuated violently, mainly in response to the U.S. need for imports; output of some minerals (iron ore, manganese, and nickel) rose in World War II but fell back afterwards and only recovered again in the course of the 1950's. The index of manufacturing output rose by no more than 20 percent between 1947 and 1957, and showed setbacks whenever sugar did.

Although the economic statistics are not firm enough to permit much confidence to be placed in them, especially for the years before 1947, the general impression they give is unmistakable. It is one of chronic stagnation from the 1920's onwards in real per capita income. The upward trend in income barely kept pace with the rise in population, which averaged rather more than two percent a year between the censuses of 1919 and 1943. The very tentative estimates of Alienes indicate that the end-of-war boom of 1944–47 hardly brought average real incomes back to the levels of corresponding years for the previous war (1916–19).

There is some confirmation of the general failure of

per capita real incomes to rise from the 1920's to the 1940's in data given in an Economic Commission for Latin America study of consumption trends, based on statistics of local output and imports. The statistical raw material, even on such important, easily measured items, is suspect; but when many series all tell broadly the same story and tell it in a vivid manner, then one can trust this story much more than any of the individual series. . . . From 1905–09 to 1925–29, consumption of basic foods seemed at least to keep pace with the population; but, though the rate of advance of population slowed down in the next two decades, the expansion of consumption showed an even greater deceleration. In these twenty years, the consumption only of wheat flour and beans kept roughly in line with the population (and only beer consumption rose faster). The leveling-off in the trends of energy and transport consumption was especially marked. The pace of growth of output quickened somewhat in the 1950's, especially in the Korean war boom of 1951–52, and again in the Suez crisis of 1956–57. But the population growth had also accelerated (to 2.5 percent a year) and in 1958 per capita real income was still only about the same as it had been in 1947.

Further information which is consistent with the picture of stagnant per capita income for more than three decades is the failure of large-scale unemployment to disappear after the depression. There are no figures of unemployment for the 1920's, but it must have been low, for immigration was still considerable then. On the other hand, in the period from July, 1956, to June, 1957, overt unemployment averaged 16 percent of the labor force, and this was the best year of the middle of the 1950's. Those working less than forty hours a week averaged 10 percent of the labor force in the same period, and there was also considerable disguised unemployment, especially in agriculture. Unemployment of this magnitude could hardly have appeared if there had been a big rise in per capita income (unless there was—which there was not—a great deal of mechanization).

Slowing down of economic growth to a virtual standstill was matched by a similar halt in progress in social fields. Illiteracy, after falling to relatively low levels in the first quarter of the century, failed to decline further. In fact, the proportion of children of school age attending primary school in the 1950's was lower than in the 1920's.

Cuba in the 35 years from 1923 to 1958 showed little progress. The stagnation was more serious and lasted longer than in any other Latin American economy—excepting perhaps the economies of one or two very small and poor nations such as Bolivia and Haiti. . . .

. . .

If further progress was almost impossible to achieve, the status quo in 1958 was intolerable, especially for a country so close to Florida and receiving through many channels an imposing (perhaps exaggerated) picture of North American levels of living. Income per capita per year averaged about five hundred dollars or one fifth as much as the average in the United States (far lower even than in any Southern state there). Yet by international standards this was not so bad. Only Venezuela and Argentina, of the larger Latin American countries, had a higher average income. What was intolerable was, first, a level of unemployment some three times as high as in the United States. In few families were all the male adults steadily employed. The surplus labor force lacked both legal possibilities and sufficient education to emigrate on a large scale (contrast the possibilities open to the surplus populations of two neighbors, Jamaica and Puerto Rico).

Second, in the countryside social conditions were very bad. About a third of the nation existed in squalor, eating rice, beans, bananas, and root vegetables (with hardly any meat, fish, eggs, or milk), living in huts, usually without electricity or toilet facilities, suffering from parasitic diseases and lacking access to health services, denied education (their children received only a first-grade education, if that). Particularly distressing was the lot of the *precaristas,* those squatting in makeshift quarters on public land.

A substantial fraction of the town population was also very poor. Here, too, there were squatters living in shacks, and of course there were slum tenements. In 1953 no less than one fifth of families lived in single rooms, and the average size of these families was five, according to the census. Taking the urban and the rural population together, 62 percent of the economically active population had incomes of less than $75 a month.

Moreover, the population growth had in the meantime been accelerating gradually, and was about 2.5 percent a year. The labor force was also growing, perhaps at an even faster rate. If the national product was to remain dependent on sugar and yet to increase at 2.5 percent a year, it would have been necessary to raise the average output of 1951–55 from 6,100,000 tons to over 7,000,000 tons in 1961–65 and well over 8,000,000 in 1971–75, without any deterioration in the terms of trade.

Though the pent-up demand for change was kept in check by repression of political opposition, it was very strong. Political stability can hardly be expected in a country which has fallen far behind a neighbor with which it is in close economic and political relations. In fact (and this is indicated by the surprising speed with which the armed forces of Batista collapsed) the existing state of affairs—in which people were short of food and work but land lay idle and factories were not built—could not continue.

Suggestions for Additional Reading

The most detailed and extensive history of all phases of Cuba's development is the ten-volume *Historia de la nación cubana,* by Ramiro Guerra y Sánchez, José M. Pérez Cabrera, Juan J. Remos, Emeterio S. Santovenia, and others. Dated, but still useful for the colonial period is Ramiro Guerra y Sánchez, *Manual de historia de Cuba (económica, social, y política), desde su descubrimiento hasta 1868* (Havana, 1938). Until quite recently the only survey of Cuban history available in English was the five-volume study which W. F. Johnson published in 1920. This gap is being filled by Philip I. Foner, *A History of Cuba and Its Relations With the United States* (New York, 1961–63); Vol. I covers the period 1492–1845, and Vol. II extends the coverage to 1895. Light but useful books about Cuban life are: Erna Fergusson, *Cuba* (New York, 1946), Hudson Strode, *The Pageant of Cuba* (New York, 1934), and Irene A. Wright, *Cuba* (New York, 1912); the latter work has numerous insights into the problems of modern Cuba. A very useful one-volume introduction to Cuban culture generally is Wyatt MacGaffey and Clifford R. Barnett, *Cuba: Its People, Its Society, Its Culture* (New Haven, Conn., 1962).

One of the most vivid interpretations of the Cuban psyche is Juan Bosch's *Cuba: La isla fascinante* (Santiago de Chile, 1955). Combining economic history and sociology, Fernando Ortiz has written one of the classic interpretations of the development of Cuban culture and society in his *Cuban Counterpoint: Tobacco and Sugar* (New York, 1947); the volume was first published in Havana in 1940. Ortiz has also stressed the mingling of diverse cultural and ethnic strains in "Los factores humanos de la cubanidad," *Revista Bimestre Cubana,* XLV (1940), pp. 165–169. Francisco Pérez de la Riva, *El Café: Historia de su cultivo y explotación en Cuba* (Havana, 1944), points out the influence of coffee production on various aspects of Cuban Life. H. E. Friedlaender, *Historia económica de Cuba* (Havana, 1944), interprets economic development to 1900 from the standpoint of the changing structure of modern capitalism.

The Indian element in early Cuban history has been studied by several scholars. Cornelius Osgood, *The Ciboney Culture of*

Cayo Redondo, Cuba (New Haven, 1942), deals with the culture of the major group of aborigines, while Fernando Ortiz, *Cuba Primitiva* (Havana, 1922), and *Historia de la arqueología cubana* (Havana, 1936), emphasizes the Spanish exploitation and elimination of the Indians. This view has been challenged by Felipe Pichardo Moya, *Los indios de Cuba en sus tiempos históricos* (Havana, 1945); this historian maintains that the Indians survived in sufficient numbers to constitute an important element of the island's present population.

Political aspects of the early colonial period may be studied in Irene A. Wright, *The Early History of Cuba: 1492–1586* (New York, 1916), and *Santiago de Cuba and its District (1607–1640)* (Madrid, 1918). Economic and social aspects are interpreted in Julio Le Riverend Brusone, *Los orígenes de la economía cubana* (Mexico, 1945), and Francisco Pérez de la Riva, *Origen y régimen de la propiedad territorial en Cuba* (Havana, 1946). Levi Marrera y Artiles, *Historia económica de Cuba: Guía de estudio y documentación* (2 vols., Havana, 1956), provides an excellent synthesis of economic developments in the sixteenth and seventeenth centuries. The basic work on slavery in Cuba is the monumental work by José Antonio Saco, *Historia de la esclavitud de la raza africana en el Nuevo Mundo y en especial en los países Américo-Hispanos* (Barcelona and Paris, 1875–1879); these are volumes IV and V of his multi-volume work on the history of slavery. A work which leans heavily on the latter, and which has a racist tone, is Hubert H. S. Aimes, *A History of Slavery in Cuba, 1511–1868* (New York, 1907).

A useful interpretive study of socio-economic development between 1763 and 1868 is Gerardo Brown Castillo, *Cuba colonial. Ensayo histórico social de la integración de la sociedad cubana* (Havana, 1952). A useful pioneering study on the development of the sugar industry and the related socio-economic problems is Ramiro Guerra y Sánchez, *Azúcar y población de las Antillas* (Havana, 1935); this volume has recently been translated and published as *Sugar and Society in the Caribbean* (New Haven, Conn., 1964). Perhaps the most definitive study of development during this period is Roland T. Ely's *Cuando reinaba su majestad el azúcar* (Buenos Aires, 1963). José L. Franco, *Política continental Americana de España en Cuba: 1812–1830* (Havana, 1947), discusses the effect of Spanish policies as the island became the base for Spanish efforts to recover the empire, and Elías Entralgo, *Los diputados por Cuba en las cortes de España durante los tres primeros períodos constitucionales* (Havana, 1945), provides the story of Cuban participation in the Spanish Cortes. A concise study of landholding may be found in Duvon C. Corbitt, "*Mercedes* and *Realengos:* A Survey of the Public Land System in Cuba," *Hispanic American Historical Review,* XIX (1939), and the same author's *The Colonial Government of Cuba* (Chapel Hill, N.C., 1938) is a useful political study.

A most voluminous bibliography exists for the nineteenth century struggles for independence. Various aspects and interpretations can be found in Roque E. Garrigó, *Historia documentada de la Conspiración de los Soles y Rayos de Bolívar* (Havana, 1939); Raúl Cepero Bonilla, *Azúcar y Abolición: Apuntes para una historia crítica del abolicionismo* (Havana, 1948); Diego González, *Historia documentada de los Movimientos Revolucionarios por la Independencia de Cuba, 1852–1867* (2 vols., Havana, 1939); and, Herminio Portell Vilá, *Narciso López y su época* (2 vols., Havana, 1930–1958). The two latter books argue that López was not an annexationist or a mere filibusterer. For the Ten Years War three of the best studies are Francisco J. Ponte Domínguez, *Historia de la Guerra de los Diez Años* (2 vols., Havana, 1944, 1958); Ramiro Guerra y Sánchez, *Guerra de los Diez Años, 1868–1878* (2 vols., Havana, 1950); and Elías Entralgo, *La Insurrección de los Diez Años. Una interpretación social de este fenómeno histórico* (Havana, 1950).

The revolution which started in 1895, and which provoked U.S. intervention, has sparked a heated debate. Herminio Portell Vilá, *Historia de la guerra de Cuba y los Estados Unidos contra España* (Havana, 1949), and Emilio Roig de Leuchsenring, *La guerra Cubano-Hispanoamericana fué ganada por el Lugarteniente General del Ejército Libertador Calixto García Iñiguez* (Havana, 1955) present the Cuban emphasis and challenge many traditional, North American views. Rufino Pérez Landa, *Bartolomé Masó y Márquez: Estudio biográfico documentado* (Havana, 1947), is highly critical of those Cubans who co-operated with the U.S.; while Cosme de la Torriente, *Fin de la dominación de España en Cuba* (Havana, 1948), argues for the necessity of U.S. intervention. The standard U.S. version is recorded in Walter Millis, *The Martial Spirit: A Study of the War With Spain* (New York, 1931), and Frank Freidel, *The Splendid Little War* (Boston, 1958). A fascinating little book by a U.S. veteran presents a generally more accurate view of the war in 1898 than the scholarly tomes: see Charles J. Post, *The Little War of Private Post* (Boston, 1961).

For the first two and a half decades of the twentieth century a useful political survey is Charles E. Chapman's *A History of the Cuban Republic: A Study in Hispanic American Politics* (New York, 1927). Economic aspects are analyzed in Henry C. Wallich, *Monetary Problems of an Export Economy: The Cuban Experience, 1914–1947* (Cambridge, Mass., 1950); Gustavo Gutiérrez, *El desarrollo económico de Cuba* (Havana, 1952); Julián Alienes y Urosa, *Características fundamentales de la economía Cubana* (Havana, 1950); and Alberto Arredondo,

Cuba: Tierra indefensa (Havana, 1945). The latter book is quite antagonistic towards foreign capital. A very rosy view of economic development is presented in Grupo Cubano de Investigaciones Económicas, *Un Estudio Sobre Cuba* (Miami, Fla., 1963).

The relations between Cuba and other countries and the effect of these on Cuban development have also provoked much controversy. The most detailed study from the Cuban nationalist's point of view is the extensively researched work by Herminio Portell Vilá, *Historia de Cuba en sus relaciones con los Estados Unidos y España* (3 vols., Havana, 1938). Some of its themes are also echoed in Ramiro Guerra y Sánchez, *Cuba, Centro de rivalidad internacional en el Caribe* (Havana, 1952). Emeterio S. Santovenia, *Armonías y conflictos en torno a Cuba* (Mexico, 1956), presents a diplomatic history of Cuba as a Spanish colony. For various aspects and interpretations of U.S.–Cuban relations the following works may be consulted: Basil Rauch, *American Interest in Cuba: 1848–1855* (New York, 1948); Russel H. Fitzgibbon, *Cuba and the United States, 1900–1935* (Menasha, Wis., 1935); Leland H. Jenks, *Our Cuban Colony* (New York, 1928); Robert Freeman Smith, *The United States and Cuba: Business and Diplomacy, 1917–1960* (New York, 1960); David Healy, *The United States in Cuba, 1898–1902: Generals, Politicians, and the Search for Policy* (Madison, Wis., 1963). For a more extensive bibliography and for a broader survey see Robert Freeman Smith, *What Happened in Cuba? A Documentary History* (New York, 1963).

The best studies of philosophical currents in Cuba are Medardo Vitier, *La filosofía en Cuba* (Mexico, 1948), and Raimundo Menocal y Cueto, *Origin y desarrollo de pensamiento cubano* (2 vols., Havana, 1945–1947). Literary trends are analyzed in Juan J. Remos, *Historia de la literatura cubana* (3 vols., Havana, 1945); Salvador Bueno, *Medio siglo de literatura cubana (1902–1952)* (Havana, 1953); and José Antonio Portuondo, *El contenido social de la literatura cubana* (Mexico, 1944). The works of Fernando Ortiz dominate the field of Afro-Cuban folklore, and his findings are synthesized in *La africanía de la música folklórica de Cuba* (Havana, 1950) and *Los bailes y el teatro de los negros en el folklore de Cuba* (Havana, 1951).

Religious factors may be studied in several works, but no good survey of religion has been written. Juan Martín Leiseca's *Apuntes para la historia Eclesiástica de Cuba* (Havana, 1938) is an extremely pro-Roman Catholic volume. Gustavo Amigó, "La iglesia católica en Cuba," *Revista Joveriana,* XXVIII (1947), presents a less biased view. Some historical aspects of the Roman Catholic Church are analyzed in Leslie Dewart, *Christianity and Revolution: The Lesson of Cuba* (New York, 1963). Boris Sapir, *The Jewish Community in Cuba* (New York, 1948); Rómulo Lachatañeré, *Manuel de Santería: El sistema de cultos*

"Lucumís," (Havana, 1942); and J. Merle Davis, *The Cuban Church in a Sugar Economy* (New York, 1942), all deal with minority religious groups.

For constitutional developments the following two volumes are useful: Ramón Infiesta, *Historia constitucional de Cuba* (Havana, 1942), and Andrés María Lazcano y Marzón, *Las Constituciones de Cuba* (Madrid, 1952). An analytical study of education during the colonial period is presented in Emma Pérez, *Historia de la pedagogía en Cuba desde los orígenes hasta la guerra de independencia* (Havana, 1945).

Several good studies about the more important figures in the Cuban intellectual tradition have been written. Among these are Medardo Vitier, *La lección de Varona* (México, 1945); Roberto Agramonte y Pichardo, *José Agustín Caballero y los orígenes de la conciencia cubana* (Havana, 1952); Antonio Hernández Travieso, *El Padre Varela: Biografía del forjador de la conciencia cubana* (Havana, 1949); Raúl Lorenzo, *Sentido nacionalista del pensamiento de Saco* (Havana, 1942); and Leopoldo Horrego Estuch, *Maceo: Héroe y Carácter* (Havana, 1952). José Martí ought to be much better known in the U.S., and five good studies are: Jorge Mañach, *Martí: Apostle of Freedom* (New York, 1950); Félix Lizaso, *Martí: Martyr of Cuban Independence* (Albuquerque, N.M., 1953); Manuel Pedro González, *José Martí: Epic Chronicler of the United States in the Eighties* (Chapel Hill, N.C., 1953); Juan de Onís, (trans.), *The America of José Martí: Selected Writings* (New York, 1954); and Richard B. Gray, *José Martí: Cuban Patriot* (Gainesville, Fla., 1962).

For additional studies on Cuba the reader should consult the following specialized guides to historiography: José M. Pérez Cabrera, *Historiografía de Cuba* (Mexico, 1962); Juan J. Remos, "Historiadores de Cuba," *Revista de la Biblioteca Nacional,* VI (1955); Fermín Peraza y Sarausa, *Bibliografía martiana, 1853–1953* (Havana, 1954); and Robert Freeman Smith, "Twentieth-Century Cuban Historiography," *Hispanic American Historical Review,* XLIV (1964).

Brief Chronology of Cuban History

1510	Diego Velázquez commissioned to conquer and settle Cuba.
1533	Last major Indian resistance crushed.
1717	First revolt of the vegueros.
1728	University of Havana founded.
1762	English capture and occupation of Havana.
1790	First newspaper established.
1809	Organization by Román de la Luz of the first independence conspiracy.
1812	Conspiracy of slaves and free Negroes led by José Antonio Aponte.
1821	Organization of the Conspiracy of the Suns and Rays of Bolívar.
1825	Spanish decree gives the Captain-General of Cuba "all embracing" authority.
1837	Royal decree ends Cuban representation in the Spanish Cortes.
1844	Slave conspiracy (la Escalera) suppressed.
1849–51	Expeditions of Narciso López.
1868	"Grito de Yara"; The beginning of the Ten Years War.
1878	The Pact of Zanjón—the treaty designed to end the war. Protest of Baraguá; Antonio Maceo rejects the pact.
1879–80	*La Guerra Chiquita* (The Little War).
1886	Slavery abolished by royal decree.
1892	Cuban Revolutionary Party organized by José Martí.
1895	"Grito de Baire," The War for Independence begins; José Martí killed in battle.
1898	U.S. intervention; the war ends and the military occupation begins.
1902	The Republic of Cuba proclaimed (as limited by the Platt Amendment).
1906–09	The second U.S. intervention.
1912	The Race War.
1917–22	U.S. Marines operate in Cuba to prevent revolution.
1920	The great sugar boom collapses.
1925	Gerardo Machado becomes president.
1933	Machado ousted; the Revolt of the Sergeants; Ramón Grau San Martín becomes president.

1934	Grau San Martín ousted by Fulgencio Batista; Platt Amendment abrogated except for the Guantánamo clause. U.S. reciprocal trade agreement with Cuba, Export-Import Bank for Cuba established; the sugar marketing system established by the U.S.
1935	The general strike and student revolt crushed; Batista consolidates his power.
1940	The new constitution.
1940–44	Batista serves as president.
1944–52	Auténticos Party in power.
1952	Batista overthrows the government and returns to power.
1953	Fidel Castro organizes the attack on the Moncada Barracks in Santiago.
1956	Castro leads an expedition back to Cuba.
1959	Batista falls and the Castro era begins.

Glossary

almuerzos	luncheon meetings
Ariel	A philosophical defense of Latin American culture against the utilitarianism of the U.S., written in 1900 by José Enrique Rodó of Uruguay
Auténticos	Cuban revolutionary party organized in 1934 by several groups to carry on the ideals of the 1933 Revolution
barracones	barracks housing temporary workers; sometimes used to denote slum conditions
capas medias	middle layers of society; not a precisely defined class
caudillismo	tradition of strong-man rule; usually has military overtones
central (*centrales*)	A modern productive complex which includes a mill, cane fields, a living area for workers, and sometimes transportation facilities
continuismo	when one man holds the position of chief executive for an extended period—usually through unconstitutional methods
criada	female servant (maid)
criollo (*creole*)	A native-born Cuban of Spanish descent
cuartelazo	military uprising
"Deputy"	pen-name used by a correspondent for the *New York Times*
guajiros	A highland peasant who subsisted on a small amount of land
Antonio Guiteras	Socialist leader of the "Young Cuba" movement who played an important role in the 1933 Revolution and was murdered by Batista's agents in 1934
hacendados	owners of the larger sugar plantations
inconformes	non-conformists
ingenio	A large, steam-powered sugar mill which was developed in the latter part of the nineteenth century

Karl Christian F. Krause	German philosopher whose writings on pantheism attracted a school of Spanish followers (early nineteenth century)
Ley de Orden Público	Law of Public Order, such as the Batista government's proclamation of November, 1953, regulating political activity
monteros	huntsmen
ñáñigo	members of the secret Abkuá cult, an Afro-Cuban religious group which reputedly practiced child sacrifice
Ortodoxos	A political party formed from a split in the Auténtico party in 1946
padre bodeguero, hijo caballero, nieto pordiosero	corresponds to the slogan "Rags to riches to rags in three generations"
personalismo	A tradition in which the personality of a single leader is the major unifying factor in political parties or other movements
pistoleros	gunmen ("hoods")
Plácido	Gabriel de la Concepción Valdés, the free Negro poet executed in 1844 during the suppression of the conspiracy known as *la Escalera*
precaristas	extremely poor people living on small pieces of public land, usually the roadside
relajo	freedom to act as one pleases; a lack of social discipline
José Antonio Saco	Cuban writer and historian of the nineteenth century. Best known for his scholarly work on the history of slavery
sitieros	sedentary farmers
Miguel Tacón	Captain-General of Cuba from 1834 to 1841. Noted for his iron-handed suppression of political dissent
Father Félix Varela	A teacher at the seminary of San Carlos who, from 1811 to 1823, promulgated ideas of political reform and the abolition of slavery. He taught or inspired the nineteenth-century generations struggling for reform and independence
veguero	tobacco farmer

A NOTE ON THE TYPE

The text of this book was set on the Linotype in a face called TIMES ROMAN, designed by Stanley Morison for The Times (London), and first introduced by that newspaper in 1932.

Among typographers and designers of the twentieth century, Stanley Morison has been a strong forming influence, as typographical advisor to the English Monotype Corporation, as a director of two distinguished English publishing houses, and as a writer of sensibility, erudition, and keen practical sense.